FREEDOM, JUSTICE,
AND HOPE

TURNING POINT Christian Worldview Series
Marvin Olasky, General Editor

Turning Point: A Christian Worldview Declaration
by Herbert Schlossberg and Marvin Olasky

Prodigal Press: The Anti-Christian Bias of the American News Media
by Marvin Olasky

Freedom, Justice and Hope:
Toward a Strategy for the Poor and the Oppressed
by Marvin Olasky, Herbert Schlossberg,
Pierre Berthoud, and Clark H. Pinnock

FREEDOM, JUSTICE, AND HOPE

Toward a Strategy for the Poor and the Oppressed

Herbert Schlossberg

Pierre Berthoud

Clark H. Pinnock

Marvin Olasky, editor

CROSSWAY BOOKS • WESTCHESTER, ILLINOIS
A DIVISION OF GOOD NEWS PUBLISHERS

Freedom, Justice, and Hope

Published by Crossway Books, a division of
Good News Publishers, Westchester, Illinois 60153.

Cover illustration by Michael Garland/Image Bank.

First printing, 1988

Printed in the United States of America

Library of Congress Catalog Card Number 87-72955

ISBN 0-89107-478-3

Unless otherwise noted, all Bible quotations are from *Holy Bible: New
International Version,* copyright © 1978 by the New York International
Bible Society. Used by permission of Zondervan Bible Publishers.

T A B L E   O F

CONTENTS

FOREWORD

*S*o what?

When people write books proposing new ways of dealing with problems of international relief and development, many of us in the field are impatient. Let's just raise the money, distribute the food, and not spend our time reading books on the subject, we tend to say.

But are we spending funds in a way that truly helps man and glorifies God? Are we providing material *and* spiritual nourishment? Are we following the Bible or worshiping the idols of our age?

This book shows why development of what I would call *symbiotic ministry*—ministry not just to body or not just to soul, but to both—is essential. *Freedom, Justice, and Hope* is a first step toward rethinking all of our international relief and development work, a first step toward becoming more faithful to the Biblical mandates.

—Tetsunao Yamamori, President
Food for the Hungry International

IS THERE A WAY OUT?

Marvin Olasky

As we in America ate up our Thanksgiving leftovers last year, the sad stories began appearing in newspapers and magazines—again. "Still hungry," blared the headline over one Associated Press story.[1] "Ethiopians reap fear of famine," wailed another.[2] These were not leftover stories, but ones newly carved. Despite the 1984-1985 efforts of Western governments, charitable organizations, individual citizens, and even rock musicians, another cycle of mass starvation was under way in one of the world's saddest countries.

Flash back to the Ethiopian capital, Addis Ababa, in September 1984: Huge triumphal arches, with slogans such as "Long Live Proletarian Internationalism," stand erect in the center of the city. Big poster paintings of Marx, Engels, Lenin and Ethiopian dictator Mengistu line the streets, as the government and those loyal to it celebrate the tenth anniversary of the military coup that overthrew the old regime. Ten thousand school children, drilled by North Koreans, parade in Revolution Square holding up colored cards that spell out in Amharic "Down with Imperialism."

Addis Ababa has the look of progress in September

1984. Roads are freshly paved and buildings freshly painted. Ethiopian Airlines has just become the first airline in Africa, and only the sixth in the world, to put into commission Boeing 767s, two of them, bought for $120 million, with credit for the purchases arranged through the U.S. government-backed Export-Import Bank. A machine tools factory, a cement factory, and the "ultra-modern" Congress Hall that serves as the seat of government and is complete with a 2,000-seat cafeteria have just opened.

But there are roadblocks just outside the city.

And at the roadblocks, soldiers are turning back starving peasant farmers and their families. Men, women and children had walked for three weeks hoping to find some food—but they are not allowed to get close to the 2,000-seat cafeteria.

Journalists who begin hearing of the story learn that thousands of Ethiopians are walking in search of food, and tens of thousands more are too weak to walk. In the northern countryside nursing mothers are too malnourished to produce milk. Children lie crying on the ground, crying and dying. They are far from the 2,000-seat cafeteria.

When some journalists ask questions, the Ethiopian government denies that its economic programs have contributed to the famine. Officials blame Western countries for not sending more aid. Many in the West, particularly Christians, do respond. Food begins arriving. The International Red Cross then charges that the Ethiopian government is deliberately starving the non-Marxist peasants and diverting aid to military forces. "Either you just want to send a lot of food to the country, or you really want to help the starving," Red Cross operations director Jean

Pierre Hocke notes in February 1985: "In the second case, what is happening is unacceptable."[3]

Some food does get to those who need it. Some lives are saved. But much of what is sent, out of Western goodwill, never makes it to the starving. Probably one million Ethiopians die.

End of flashback—beginning of current dilemma. History seems to be repeating itself. What can we in America do? Our first tendency, when we hear an appeal for government or private contributions for Ethiopia, is probably to say "No." Reasons for that answer readily come to mind. Why should we come to the rescue of a government that wastes resources in such a profligate way and shoots farmers who try to act sensibly? One that suppresses trade and forcibly places its own people in collective farms that have been likened to concentration camps? Won't our aid end up hurting, by allowing the government to spend even more of its funds on centralized military and political power? What can we do when a government terrorizes its own people?

Time magazine played off Cain's question, "Am I my brother's keeper?" (Gen. 4:9), by asking, "What if my brother already has a keeper, one who has a gun and who claims the right to decide whether my brother will get any of the food I send him?"[4] *Time* quoted a U.S. relief administrator's complaint about Ethiopia's Marxist leaders: "By forcing farmers who do grow more than they consume to sell to the state at prices below the cost of production, they are not providing the incentive to produce the maximum that the land, however poor, would yield."[5] *Time* noted comments by Rony Brauman of the French charitable organization Doctors Without Borders: "The aid Ethiopians need is diplomatic pressure, not food. If we have a duty, it is to pressure the government to change its policies. Otherwise, in two or three years, we're going to see the same bodies, the same TV footage."[6]

And yet, when we look at today's footage of starving children, it affects us far more than a thousand vehement words, however true. We want desperately to do something, anything, to help. If there is a chance of support getting through, we want to try. Some negative elements creep into our thought as well: If we do not do something, anything, we feel guilty. Or perhaps the subjective act of giving is vital in itself. Is it the thought that counts?

And so we end up asking our government to send aid—"with safeguards involved," of course. And we contribute to charitable groups. We feel we have to. But we are gritting our teeth. And we'll give and grit, grit and give, again and again. The contrast between our own Thanksgiving dinner and the starving child is too great to ignore, even though we have little hope about the outcome.

But at the same time we think that there must be a better way—if not for Ethiopia this year, in the midst of famine, then for Ethiopia over the next few years, once the greatest urgency is over, and for Botswana and Burundi and Burkina Faso, for Cape Verde and Chad and the Central African Republic, for Senegal and Somalia and the Sudan, and for other countries in Africa, Asia and Latin America. Must we go from famine to famine? Liberals tend to say that more aid is the answer. Conservatives often suggest those peoples should shift for themselves. Are those the only two alternatives?

Flash back to nearly two thousand years ago. Thousands of hungry people gather around a new prophet. He teaches and heals them. Then, "Jesus called his disciples to him and said, 'I have compassion for these people; they have already been with me three days and have nothing to eat. I do not want to send them away hungry, or they may collapse on the way.' "

The disciples, thinking as materialists, ask the logical question: "Where could we get enough bread in this remote place to feed such a crowd?" They have only seven loaves and a few small fish. But Jesus tells the crowd to sit down on the ground. He takes the seven loaves and the fish, gives thanks, then breaks the food into pieces and hands them to the disciples. They in turn distribute the food to the people. Then comes one of the amazing lines of the Bible: "They all ate and were satisfied." Was this a sense of comradeship that spread among the people so that they had psychological fullness even when stomachs were distended? No, this was real food, for "Afterward the disciples picked up seven basketfuls of broken pieces that were left over." Were there perhaps not as many hungry people as there first appeared to be? No, "The number of those who ate was four thousand, besides women and children" (Matt. 15:32-38).

It is important to note that the people were fed, on real food. It is also important to note that those whose eyes were opened received sustenance far more lasting—they could also see, from Jesus' dominance over nature, that He is the Son of God. They could learn, as Jesus told His disciples, "I am the bread of life. He who comes to me will never go hungry, and he who believes in me will never be thirsty" (John 6:35).

That was an extraordinarily hard message for even the disciples, who were traveling with Jesus, to understand. They kept falling back into materialism—and so do we.

Soon after Jesus showed the nature of the world and of Himself by feeding the multitudes, He again had to castigate the disciples: "You of little faith, why are you talking among yourselves about having no bread? Do you still not understand?" (Matt. 16:8, 9).

Today, we still do not understand. Jesus turned seven loaves and a few small fish into food for thousands. We take food for thousands, send it on ships or planes to Ethiopia or other countries with full knowledge that much of it will be siphoned off, and believe we are doing the best we can when seven loaves and a few small fish get into the stomachs of those truly in need. Are such miracles-in-reverse all we have to offer? We move from Thanksgiving leftovers to the singing of Christmas carols: "Joy to the world! the Lord is come. . . . No more let sins and sorrows grow,/ Nor thorns infest the ground;/ He comes to make his blessings flow/ Far as the curse is found." We sing those words—do we mean them?

Here is a test with one main question: Why are some countries prosperous and others poor? Many American Christians will give the same materialist answer as non-Christians: Look at soil, rain, and other natural resources, examine roads and machinery, and if a country is deficient in either food or factories, transfer what is needed from rich to poor. But what about the spiritual changes that are needed to make godly use of material? Do we talk about those? And if we do, do we talk about body and soul in a dualistic manner, with economic advance and spiritual uplift seen as two activities, separate and unequal, rather than a Biblical unity?

More questions come to mind. What if we were to look hard at the Biblical assault on materialism, an assault that does not deemphasize the economic but thrusts into deeper levels of alienation, imprisonment and enslavement? What if we were to emphasize the effects of spiritual reorientation on all areas of life, with salvation, repentance, healing, and restoration revealing their visible aspects? Are such questions merely theoretical, or will concentration on them help us find ways to break the cycle of famine in many countries, and the cycle of give and grit among economically blessed Christians?

In the Spring of 1987 a group of forty evangelical Christians from around the world gathered in Villars, Switzerland, under the auspices of Food for the Hungry and the Fieldstead Institute. Our goal was to take a new look at Biblical mandates for international relief and development work. For five days we engaged in intense discussion, debate, and private reflection, our energies focused by a number of prepared study papers. This book represents an attempt to share some of that reflection with a wider group. The chapters that follow, all based on conference papers and discussion, are of wide variety, but a common denominator is the attempt to transcend materialist emphases without neglecting the mandate to provide real bread as well as spiritual bread to those in need.

Three images remain in my mind from the consultation. First, I remember Udo Middelmann of the International Institute for Relief and Development, a brilliant speaker, looking out at night over the lights of Rhone River valley villages from our meeting place high in the Alps. He told of the long history of the valley, of Hannibal with his army and elephants marching through it, of early settlers fearing the mountain gods, but of the Swiss century by century turning inhospitable areas into pleasant places indeed. Contemplating the sweep of history does not allow us to forget the crushing needs of today, but it does remind us how life can and does change over time, and how poverty can be turned into prosperity.

A second image in my mind is of Ted Yamamori, head of Food for the Hungry, telling of an African girl dying, with the girl's mother saying, "It is fated that she should die," and Ted saying, "No, it is not." When the girl received adequate medical attention she did not die. Perhaps, among some people, a bit of their fatalism did die. Physical renewal and a change in worldviews could go together.

A third image that remains is of the assembled Christian leaders at the end of one long discussion, where many perspectives had been presented and some important but wearisome wrangling about the relation of law and grace had just ended. The person selected to close us with prayer had a hard task, since sometimes prayers can be used as weapons. What words would he choose? Would he lean to one side or another? That person chose—the Holy Spirit chose for him—the best words of all, and as he spoke all of us joined in: "Our Father who art in heaven, hallowed be thy name. Thy kingdom come, thy will be done, in earth as it is in heaven. Give us this day our daily bread. . . ."

This book is more a prayer than a textbook. It does not pretend to be in any way comprehensive. Instead, it tries to open up what we hope will be a fundamental debate on Biblical mandates for relief and development. For example, the next chapter does not review all of the Old Testament thinking concerning poverty and oppression, but gives a close reading to passages in Genesis and Amos that help to put the social prophets in covenant context. Chapters 3 and 4 do not critique all of the theories favoring governmental economic power in fighting poverty, but look closely at the arguments and presuppositions of a leading collectivist and at the practice of Marxism. Chapters 5 and 6 evaluate the work of a leading critic of governmental economic control and add specific detail concerning the imperatives of economic development. Chapter 7 brings out other aspects of the conference and some current applications, and Chapter 8 presents a succinct summary, "The Villars Statement on Relief and Development," that conference participants signed.

This book does not follow the typical format of the TURNING POINT Christian Worldview Series: single-authored books, with comprehensive analysis. This book is more evocative and tentative. But if the twenty-first century is to be a better one for the oppressed than the twentieth, Christians cannot wait for every jot and tittle of analysis to be in place. "When he saw the crowds, he had compassion on them, because they were harassed and helpless" (Matt. 9:36). Jesus had such compassion that He would give His life for all of us who recognize that we are harassed and helpless. In our helplessness, we want to begin an effort to help today's harassed.

PROPHET AND COVENANT

Pierre Berthoud

One of the most quoted books of the Bible in regard to issues of international relief and development is the book of Amos. Amos vigorously pleads for the poor and criticizes those who "lie on beds inlaid with ivory" and "dine on choice lambs" (Amos 6:4). But we have to be careful to read these comments not through twentieth-century eyes heavily influenced, consciously or unconsciously, by Marxist and other materialist perspectives.

In order to apply properly the prophetic insights of Amos, it is essential first to understand his message in light of the historical situation of Amos, and in light of the central theological theme of the Old Testament—namely, God's eternal covenant with man. With this understanding clearly in mind, we can then apply the insights of Amos to the situation of the poor and the oppressed.

Biblically, the covenant is a treaty that God, the ruler, has concluded with man, the subject. It establishes that man is not autonomous and implies that the creature is responsible before the Creator who has given "all men life and breath and everything else" (Acts 17:25). Although Amos does not use the word "covenant," the concept nevertheless underlies and permeates his message and his vision of reality. In the oracles of the shepherd of Tekoa, the covenant has a double dimension: It is both creational and redemptional. This essay shows how an understanding of both aspects is essential to developing a Biblical view of relief and development.

THE COVENANT OF CREATION

First, we should discuss Amos' praise of the Creator-God, "He who forms the mountains, creates the wind, and reveals his thoughts to man, he who turns dawn to darkness, and treads the high places of the earth" (4:13).[1] The covenant of creation (also known as the covenant of works or of life), one of the pillars of the Biblical perspective, is presented in the first three chapters of Genesis and renewed within a fallen world in the treaty that God established with Noah and his sons (Gen. 9:8-17). Here are some of the characteristics of the covenant, as set forth early in Genesis:

—The Lord Himself is the initiator of His covenant of life. He is the God of Heaven and earth, the ultimate reality. Though infinite, God is also a personal being: He thinks, loves and acts.

—All things are dependent upon God. By establishing the fundamental Creator-creature motif, God specifies the nature of the relation man is to have with God and with the universe.

—Precise stipulations are given, the respect or rejection of which are sanctioned by God's blessing or curse. Man has God-given liberty to eat of the fruit of the earth (Gen. 2:8, 15, 16) and to exercise dominion over the creatures (Gen. 1:28). God ordains marriage, with the promise of families (Gen. 2:18). Most importantly, God offers man communion with Himself (Gen. 1:26-29; 3:8) and thus introduces the Sabbath.

—God, in summary, enters into a covenant of life with man, upon condition of personal and perpetual obedience (Gal. 3:12; Rom. 10:5). The tree of life was token of the covenant (Gen. 2:9); eating of the tree of the knowledge of good and evil, however, would lead to the pain of death (Gen. 2:17).[2]

It is vital to remember that the Lord, not man, initiates this covenant; its scope is universal. The covenant requires obedience of not just some men but all men, because Adam, the head of the human race, is representative of mankind as a whole (Rom. 5:12-21). When the Bible tells us that man is created[3] in the "image of God" (Gen. 1:26, 27), we are given two pieces of information vital to understanding how we are to respond to suffering around the world: We are told about the nature of man —all men and women—and we are told about the position or function of man in creation.

We are told about the nature of man in that the word "*image* of God" means effigy or representation (1 Sam. 6:5; 2 Kings 11:18; Ezek. 23:14). For the ancients, an image had worth in relation to the object or person that it resembles. This means that man is to define himself with reference to God, and that his primary calling is to be in fellowship with God. This expression also conveys the idea of sonship, an idea found in Luke's genealogy of Jesus when Adam is declared "son of God" (Luke 3:38). The Apostle Paul conveys the same thought when he says: "We are his offspring" (Acts 17:28).[4]

Emphasizing the vertical dimension does not mean embracing a soul/body dualism.[5] The Bible emphasizes the unity of man: Man does not have a body, he is a body. Supposedly feeding the soul while starving the body leaves us with a corpse. But it is important to avoid the common tendency today to reduce man to a purely horizontal dimension. The expression "image of God" underscores the uniqueness of man. Yes, he is "of the earth," and is one among many creatures, yet he is a being who like God thinks, loves and acts; man is qualitatively different from the rest of creation.[6] He is a spiritual being called to live a conscious relationship with his ultimate partner, a relationship which transcends his body without reducing its value.

The expression "image of God" also suggests man's calling: God created the world, and man can exercise dominion over it. Psalm 8, while using the vocabulary of enthronement to stress the greatness and dignity of man, reiterates the cultural mandate found in Genesis: "Subdue [the earth]. Rule over the fish of the sea and the birds of the air and over every living creature that moves on the ground" (Gen. 1:28). The same idea is emphasized in a different way in the narrative dealing with Adam and Eve in the Garden of Eden: "The Lord God took the man and put him in the Garden of Eden to work it and take care of it" (Gen 2:15).

The first chapter of Genesis emphasizes the *subjection*[7] of creation. Man, the unique creature, the climax of God's creative activity, is given authority, under God. But the second chapter adds a nuance as if to anticipate the possible misuse of power. Rather than tyrannizing creation, man is "to serve it."[8] When man exploits the earth, he must look after that with which God has entrusted him. When man works "for the king" (Ps. 45:1), work can become a "form of worship." Though man is unique in dignity, he is not autonomous. He is responsible for his stewardship before the Creator. He is to "take care of"[9] the creation with the same solicitude the Father shows toward His handiwork (Prov. 8:30, 31; Rom. 8:18-22).

That position of authority under a God who sets specific limits contrasts with the pattern of ancient oriental despotism, where in practice the tyrant's power was unlimited. The Biblical view contrasts with ancient pagan mentalities in another way also: The Babylonians saw work as negative, something thrust upon men by lazy gods, but the early chapters of Genesis portray work and labor in a positive light. The statement, "Be fruitful and increase in number; fill the earth and subdue it" (Gen. 1:28) implies both numeric and economic growth. Though all things belong to God, ownership and the right to property are clearly implied.[10]

MAN'S CULTURAL MANDATE WITHIN A BROKEN WORLD

Chapters 4 through 6 of Genesis deal specifically with the development of the human race rather than with the history of redemption, and thus show us how man began to fill the earth and subdue it. Abel and Cain were involved in agriculture, and Cain later built a permanent settlement (4:1, 17).[11] Jabal was the father of the semi-nomadic herders of livestock (4:20); Jubal was the father of musicians and therefore of culture as a whole (4:21); Tubal-Cain, half-brother of Jabal and Jubal, was the father of technology and industry (4:22). These names and chronologies, so often skipped over in Bible reading, show a crucial distinctive of the Biblical worldview: Israel's neighbors ascribed the organization of civilization to the gods,[12] but Genesis shows that civilization and culture were constructed by mortal men created after the image of God. Genesis continually stresses the dignity and worth of man who is capable of creative imagination.

Again, just as the earlier chapters of Genesis anticipate the misuse of power, so we should remember here that it is the line of Cain that is doing all these things. That lineage is not an outright condemnation of man's civilizing action, but post-Fall activities always have a note of ambiguity. What is the meaning of civilization and culture for the creature who has become his own finality? Will not stewardship be transformed into a drive for autonomy? The rebellion of the first couple[13] led to an alienation that spread to every area of life both on a vertical and horizontal level: alienation from God, self, fellowman, all the other creatures. The murders committed by Cain and Lamech, along with the advent of tyranny and polygamy (Gen. 4:19), illustrate in a striking fashion the dynamic and the expansion of sin.

And yet, after all of this abuse of power, and after God's judgment of that abuse by means of the great flood, He graciously renews His covenant. The treaty He concludes with Noah introduces a time of patience, with a view to the realization of God's plan of redemption (Rom. 3:25; 8:18-25). The covenant, given despite the wickedness of man's heart—thoughts, emotions and actions—is established by God alone. It is universal, including in its scope not only Noah, but also his descendants, all other creatures, and even the whole earth (Gen 9:9-13). It is not conditioned by obedience to specific stipulations, and it is for "as long as the earth endures" (Gen 8:22). The rainbow, as the sign of the covenant, guarantees cosmic stability (Gen. 9:8-18) and testifies to the faithfulness and patience of God.[14]

It is within this framework that man's cultural mandate is renewed (Gen. 9:1-8). In the midst of a reality that suffers the consequences of evil, things are not quite the same. Dominion over the other creatures arouses "fear and dread" (Gen. 9:2). In addition to "green plants," men may now eat "everything that lives and moves" as long as the blood has been removed (Gen. 9:3, 4).[15] God Himself introduces capital punishment: "Whoever sheds the blood of man, by man shall his blood be shed; for in the image of God has God made man" (Gen. 9:6). Indeed, the very nature of the Lord is the ultimate foundation of right. To recognize that nature and abide by it is a safeguard against all forms of arbitrary action. God gives man liberty under Himself, and establishes justice for all.

THE COVENANT OF REDEMPTION

That is what God does for everyone. But he also does particular things for a particular people. As M. H. Segal notes, "The real theme of the Pentateuch is the selection of Israel from the nations and its consecration to the service of God and his laws in a divinely-appointed land."[16] God promises to make the descendants of Abraham into the people of God and to give them Canaan as an everlasting inheritance (Gen. 15; 17:7, 8). God also makes a third promise, stated explicitly in His call to Abram: "All peoples on earth will be blessed through you" (Gen. 12:3). That promise clearly emphasizes both the redemptional and universal scope of God's purpose: God's original blessing on all mankind (Gen. 1:28) would be restored through Abraham and his descendants, reaching fulfillment in the person and work of the Messiah.

Israel's task is to glorify God by demonstrating His holiness in the midst of a lost world. By the means of a particular people, divine beauty, truth, and redemption will shine forth among men as they lie in the shadow of death. As the Lord, who has delivered His people out of Egyptian bondage, declares to Moses just before the revelation on Sinai, "Out of all nations . . . you will be for me a kingdom of priests and a holy nation" (Exod. 19:4-6). Israel, "the kingdom of priests," is to be to the nations of the world what the priests are to a nation: leaders of worship, teachers of truth.

God makes known to His "treasured possession" (v. 5) the law by which they must live. Rather than exalting man's discretion, that law carefully limits arrogant power. It proclaims, among other things, that human life is sacred, that all men are equal before God, and that the weaker members of the community must be protected and defended.

Those distinctives need emphasis, because the Biblical view of law is very different from that found in other ancient codes. In Mesopotamia the law was above the gods; they functioned as its witnesses, defenders and guardians. In Israel, with the law incorporated into the covenant, God is the author, source and fountain of law. The Psalmist expressed this understanding well by writing, "He has revealed his word to Jacob, his laws and decrees to Israel. He has done this for no other nation; they do not

know his laws" (Ps. 147:19, 20). The law, far from imper-
sonal, was a statement of God's will, and was to govern the
whole of life.[17]

Furthermore, in Mesopotamia the king alone was chosen by the gods to receive the perception of truth. In Israel,
however, the law was given and proclaimed to the community as a whole (Exod. 21:1). It was not the prerogative of a
class of professionals (jurist, lawyer, judge); the law was
read publicly to the people every seven years. Both individual and social responsibility were emphasized. Everyone
could know the rule that he who destroys human life is
accountable for the crime committed (Exod. 21:12). A
murderer was not supposed to be able to buy his way out
or use his power to escape justice, for religious values
precede economic or political considerations. The corollary
also was true: The death penalty was suppressed in the case
of crimes committed against property, regardless of whose
property was taken.

Similarly, the principle that all men are equal before
God was of fundamental importance. In principle, there
was no class justice in Israel as there is in the Code of
Hammurabi.[18] Those in power were not to suspend the
rules for their own benefit. The famous "eye for eye, tooth
for tooth" verse, so often misunderstood, limited the punishment to the person committing the offense, and specified that the penalty must correspond to the crime perpe-
trated.[19] Significantly, the Bible provided not for survival of
the fittest, but for protection of the the weaker members of
the community: the blind and the deaf (Deut. 27:18), widows and orphans (Deut. 27:17-22), the foreigner (Deut.
27:17; Exod. 23:6), the poor (Deut. 15:7-11; Exod. 23:6),
the debtor who sells himself into slavery (Deut. 15:12-18),

and those born slaves (Exod. 23:12). The law requires that they be protected from oppression and exploitation. Even their specific prerogatives are indicated (Deut. 14:29).

In summary, the five books of Moses show concern for justice for all mankind, with the idea of justice always couched within the covenant and resting upon theocentric thought.[20] Israel has the task of being a light unto the Gentiles, showing God's way of ministering to both body and soul. Now, with these aspects of the covenant established, we may approach within Biblical thought-patterns the message that Amos delivered to Judah and Israel.

AMOS IN CONTEXT

To begin with, we will touch on the historical background. Living during the eighth century B.C., Amos prophesied during the reigns of Jeroboam II (786-746), king of Israel, and Azariah (also named Uzziah, 783-742), king of Judah. He probably began his public ministry towards the middle of the century. For both kingdoms, it was a time of security, peace and political growth. Previously, Aram (Syria) had continually made inroads upon Israel and had even invaded its territory on a number of occasions. But with the rise of Assyria, the Syrian power had been broken; Adadnirari III's conquest of Damascus precipitated Aram into a period of weakness which was to benefit both the Northern and the Southern kingdoms.

Assyria would eventually conquer Israel, but during this period the Assyrian armies were occupied with various internal and external dangers. It is therefore not surprising that Israel and Judah, though divided, gained back the territory lost after the death of Solomon. Jeroboam II in-

cluded in his sphere of influence Aram and Hamath to the
north and Ammon and Moab to the east. Uzziah extended
the boundaries of Judah to include Edom, the tribes of
Arabia, the Negev and the Philistine cities (Gath, Jabnet
and Ashdod). Key trade routes—one following the coast-
line, another going through Transjordania—once again
passed through both kingdoms. The Phoenician cities of
Tyre and Sidon offered an opening onto the Mediterra-
nean, while the port of Elath, on the Red Sea, became an
important channel for trade with partners in the south.[21]
As Neher wrote, "Palestine, cross-roads of the sea and the
land routes, becomes the center of international economic
exchanges."[22]

In addition to the renewal of trade, industrial activities
flourished,[23] herds grew, and agriculture was encouraged.[24]
The era of peace and prosperity was not limited to the
royal house, but extended to a wealthy class of society
mainly made up of the nobility, officers and merchants.
Those individuals built magnificent houses and invested in
costly furniture (probably made in Damascus[25]) and ivory
ornaments (often inlaid with precious stones such as lapis-
lazuli). The well-being of this upper-class, described by
Amos, has been confirmed by archaeological finds made in
Samaria.[26]

Amos never condemns prosperity that results from
honest, hard work, or from wise investment of wealth. He
attacks shameless business practices such as "skimping the
measure, boosting the price and cheating with dishonest
scales" (Amos 8:5). He attacks those who ignore the misery
around them and instead practice a superficial optimism,
particularly in international relations (Amos 6:1-7). Freed

from the immediate threat of powerful Aram, Israel and Judah did not see, or pretended not to see, the danger that was rising in the north. Having made new gods for themselves alongside the God of the covenant, enjoying the comfort that wealth and well-being bring, they did not recognize the fatal consequences of sin.

Israel and Judah also did not understand the cause of their prosperity. Instead of ascribing economic success to the mercy of God and their forefathers' development of a Biblical worldview concerning economics, they often gave thanks to Baal, god of storms and controller of fertility within the Canaanite and Phoenician cults.[27] Such idol worship obviously was a direct affront to God. In Baal worship, as in other pagan myths, evil is part of the ultimate make-up of reality—that is, God—and absolute right and wrong do not exist. In paganism, with its naturalistic emphasis, history is replaced by an endless repetition of the cycles of cosmic life, and man is only a part of them; therefore, the significance and meaning of history and of man is greatly reduced. If there is ultimately no personal absolute in the universe, what is evil and why fight it? In the light of these considerations, one can understand why the prophets denounced with such vigor all forms of idolatry. Baalism presented powerless gods (with the limitations and sins common to man) and demanded that they be adored. Baalism thus explained the world in a way totally contradicting the Bible (1 Kings 18:16-45).

Despite the syncretism, God did not turn his back on His people. He did not even ignore those who were not His people, because other nations were also accountable before God. As Paul would later write, "the wrath of God is being revealed from heaven against all the godlessness and wickedness of men who suppress the truth by their wickedness" (Rom. 1:18ff.).

THE GENERAL REQUIREMENTS

On the basis of the covenant of creation established with Adam and renewed with Noah and his descendants, Amos criticizes Syria, Philistia, Phoenicia, Edom, Ammon and Moab. For example, Amos speaks out against the *brutal inhumanity* that Syria shows in warfare: "Damascus has threshed Gilead with sledges having iron teeth" (Amos 1:3). He attacks the Philistine deportation of civilians, innocent refugees destined to become merchandise in the international marketplace (Amos 1:6; see also Joel 3:8; Obad. 20). He protests the self-interested Phoenician betrayal of the "treaty of brotherhood" with Israel (Amos 1:9; 1 Kings 5:26; 9:14). He denounces the savage acts of cruelty perpetuated in order to expand territory. Thus, "Ammon . . . ripped open the pregnant women of Gilead in order to extend his borders" (Amos 1:13).

Amos, in short, attacks those who do not respect a key fact of Genesis 1: Man is made "in the image of God." To hate the image-bearer is to hate the image, so Amos attacks the "stifling [of] all compassion" (Amos 1:11) and the violent anger that seeks to obliterate the very last trace of one's enemies. For example, God sends fire on Moab "because he burned, as if to lime, the bones of Edom's king" (Amos 2:1).[28] Neher's translation of that verse—"because Moab has burned the bones left by the king of Edom in order to extract lime"—brings up another point: Was Edom using corpses abandoned on the battlefield for industrial purposes, thus placing economic considerations above the honor due to a man's memory?[29] It is difficult to decide which is the better interpretation, but both are an expression of an utter contempt for man. God condemns that contempt for those made after His image, whether they are from Israel or from other nations.

In his commentary on Amos, A. Motyer draws, from the passage we have been dealing with, principles of conduct which are valid for both individuals and communities: Man is not an object that can be manipulated as one sees fit; truth and loyalty in human relationships and affairs are crucial; seeking for power and money must be checked by ethical standards; all humans deserve respect.[30] It is important to note that these principles are couched in a worldview that corresponds basically to the Noahic covenant: Man is unique; he lives in a moral universe; he is accountable to God, the ultimate absolute. That is why Amos argues with such vigor against arbitrary power of all kinds: He sees man's dictatorship as the very negation of the meaningfulness of God's universe, and an attack on God Himself!

It is not difficult to see the relevance of such a message to questions of international relief and development. First, man is a responsible creature. According to a rabbinic exegesis of the famous recurring verse in Amos, God is saying, "Because of the three sins of Damascus, of Gaza . . ., because of four, I will not bring back Damascus, Gaza . . . from the destiny it has brought upon itself by its sins and which I had forgiven on many occasions" (1:3, 6, 9, 11, 13; 2:1).[31] Though it is a fearful thing to fall into the hands of a holy God, choice is a decisive factor in the disaster and ruin that came upon these nations. Man can operate within the covenant given to Noah and take dominion, or man can arrogantly bring about poverty and destruction. There is no place here for a deterministic view of history and culture.

Secondly, Amos also reminds us that God's judgment is both a call to repentance and a vindication and protection of the humble. The justice and the solicitude of the Father are for those who have been "threshed" (Amos 1:3), led into captivity (1:6), or betrayed (1:9); it is for those who are the object of sinful anger (1:11), sickening violence (1:13), and unjust commercial transactions (1:6, 9; 2:1). God is the uncompromising advocate of those who are victims of the violations of the law He has given for the well-being of His creatures. Nevertheless, within the Biblical perspective, poverty, misery and suffering have no value in themselves. They are also related to man's decision-making significance, and can be the consequence of irresponsible and often unwise choices.

A third aspect relates to the role of God's chosen people—chosen for special grace but also special work, to be a nation of priests in service to the world. Amos' first six oracles deal with nations under the Noahic Covenant but not the Mosaic; the final two deal specifically with Judah and Israel, and we should now examine them.

THE PARTICULAR REQUIREMENTS

The prophet begins by placing the spotlight upon Judah. It is found guilty, even more so than the surrounding nations, for it has been the object of God's solicitude and special revelation. Indeed, the kingdom has rejected the teaching of God in nature and history; it has broken away from the religious and moral precepts of the covenant. Judah has abandoned the wisdom of God in order to follow the deviations of the false and deceitful gods (Amos 2:4). In practice, to turn to the idols and to seek their help is the equivalent of pushing God out of one's mental horizon. Exaltation of self is at the heart of rebellion against God and inevitably leads to despising His will.[32]

The northern kingdom is in even worse shape. At the time of the schism, Jeroboam I established two new sanctuaries, Dan in the north and Bethel in the south, so that the people would not have to go to Jerusalem and thus fall under the influence of the kingdom of Judah. Jereboam I introduced into his new state-church the calf symbol of power and fertility; he said it was to represent the Lord, but he was introducing a pagan symbol into the worship of God.[33] In addition, the king assumed the function of high priest and appointed non-Levitical priests to preside over the new religion and worship (1 Kings 12:28-33). Apparently he forgot history and the dramatic consequences of wanting to identify the Lord with the golden calf (Exod. 32).

Amos couches his attack upon both Judah and Israel in a framework of covenant. In his oracle against the inhabitants of Judah, Amos recalled that they had been given the law (Amos 2:4); in his statement against Israel he evoked God's past blessings. The two oracles taken together refer to elements that constitute a covenant: the deliverance from Egypt (Amos 2:10), the bestowing of a constitution (2:4), and the giving of a land (2:9). Though divided, the two nations belong to the same body: They have both benefited from God's solicitude, and they are both responsible before Him for deliberately disregarding His will and following vain idols created out of their supposedly autonomous imagination.

Both Judah and Israel, in short, were playing down the

requirements of God and pretending that moral life and
economic success could be gained by reliance on gods
embodied in the fluctuating forces of nature and in the
capricious will of man. This meant, whatever the quality of
the religious makeup, that man became the measure of all
things on both the individual and institutional level. Proclaiming freedom from all checks and balances, autonomy
led the people of the covenant to discover the reverse side
of significance. Their selfish desires, interests, and utopias
became the norms of their judicial, economic, political,
diplomatic and military activities. They sought new security in the self-sufficient virtues of royal authority, diplomacy,
and military power.

Such a perversion yielded only bitterness, violence, and
death. Egoism, arbitrary force and ruthless exploitation
blunted moral judgment and undermined social justice and
peace. It is precisely at this moment in history that one
finds a deep fissure in the social tissue of Judah/Israel. As
guardian of the covenant, Amos identified specific evils,
including the corruption of the law-courts so that they did
not defend the cause of the innocent and of the defenseless
(Amos 2:6; 8:6), but merely responded to personal power.[34]
Not only were the innocent and the defenseless despised,
but in the case of a misdeed, the penalty did not correspond to the crime committed. Two of the specific tenets
of Biblical law—equal justice for all, and consideration for
the weak—were set aside.

Those who had power forced ruthless economic practices that respected neither the person made in the image of
God nor the property of the powerless (Amos 2:6; 8:6).
The "poor" are considered righteous not because of their
economic position as such, but because they are both inno-

cent and defenseless.[35] Peasants were compelled to surrender their crops at their own expense (Amos 5:11a). Prosperity based on wrongful gain flourished, with those newly-rich through use of power eager to invest in land and real estate (Amos 3:15; 5:11b). Amos never champions poverty against prosperity—such an opposition is foreign to the Biblical mentality—but he questions the acquisition of wealth at the expense of the respect for God's law and therefore of justice. He attacks the way that Judah and Israel threw off the just requirements of the covenant and based their conduct on the desires and inclinations of their fickle hearts (Amos 3:9b; 8:5, 6).

The oppression is such that weaker members of the community are disregarded or simply brushed aside (Amos 2:7a; 8:4a), while the Nazarite and the prophets, guardians of the covenant, are encouraged to betray their calling and deny their ministry (Amos 2:12). The words of Paul describing the godless generation in the last days are quite fitting for the contemporaries of Amos: they are "lovers of pleasure rather than lovers of God" (2 Tim. 3:4). This is true both of the inhabitants of Samaria—including some of the wealthy women (Amos 4:1)—and of Judah who seem to be totally unaware that calamity is at hand (Amos 6:1-6; 5:18). They have opted for a short-sighted philosophy of life. Since life and death have no ultimate meaning, "let us eat and drink, for tomorrow we die" (1 Cor. 15:32).[36] Man has no ultimate purpose; he is alone in a universe which is amoral and arbitrary!

It is therefore not surprising that the Israelites showed disdain for God, for His will, for His servants, and for true worship. God's special people were as insensitive as all the other nations—even more so, because they were insensitive to God's working among them. They considered the day of the coming of the Lord as a day of light and not of darkness (Amos 5:18). They did not grieve over the imminent ruin of their country (Amos 6:6). They refused to hear the oracles of the prophet (7:16). They would not reflect on the disastrous consequences of their acts as God sought to bring them back from their evil ways (4:6-11). They acted so horribly because they had become ungodly, profaning God Himself by despising His covenant. Amos eloquently linked religious infidelity and social injustice by noting that "Father and son use the same girl and so profane my holy name. They lie down beside every altar on garments taken in pledge. In the house of their gods they drink wine taken as fines" (Amos 2:7b, 8).

In this passage, the shepherd of Tekoa exposed immorality, probably the sacred prostitution that was at the heart of the fertility cult (v. 7b) and the ill-gotten gains used to promote religious idolatry (v. 8)[37] It is clear here, as elsewhere in the prophecy, that government-backed creeds had become a means to an end, that of justifying the wickedness of man's heart. Amos attacks religious formalism and hypocrisy that deny justice and righteousness (Amos 5:21-24; 8:4), Canaanite idolatry (Amos 2:7b, 8; 5:26), and also the propensity to adapt the ritual and its meaning to the circumstances at hand.[38]

Israel, in short, thought it could worship the gods as well as the Lord. Such confusion could lead only to the denial of the one true God and the advent of a man-made religion (Amos 4:5; 6:8; 7:9). This arrogant pride blinded Israelites and led to a change in their whole outlook and system of values. It made them despise truth and run after lies, hate good and love evil (Amos 5:15). And yet, what weight could the creature-god carry in comparison with the Creator-Judge, the moral absolute and fountain of life, the God who holds the universe in His power?

CONCLUSION

Amos announced imminent disaster, the result of responsible choice, but through words of judgment he sought to awaken the consciences of his listeners and thus open the way of redemption. Clouds were thick on the horizon, but there was still time to repent. That is why the prophet appealed untiringly to the responsibility of the covenant people (Amos 4:4; 5:5, 6, 14, 15), confronting them with a choice between God and idols, between God and man, between God and nothingness, between truth and falsehood, between good and evil, between life and death. Sadly, Israel did not heed the warnings of Amos. It brought upon itself invasion and exile, the consequences of its decisions. Judah, after a reprieve, suffered the same calamities.

In the midst of turmoil, however, God was watching over his wide and gracious design. His promise of salvation is couched in Amos' last oracle (Amos 9:8-15), which begins by identifying the imminent judgment with an act of purification (vv. 9, 10). Although destruction was to overcome the kingdoms of Judah and Israel, God would establish His kingdom of peace and prosperity by means of a remnant. The Lord would undertake the restoration of the house of David, the messianic kingdom (2 Sam. 7) that would extend to all the nations, to all those who would be the objects of divine grace.[39] This promise began to be fulfilled with the return from exile, but more significantly with the coming of Jesus of Nazareth.

That is the grand message of Amos, a book that should

not be turned into a narrow tract. To read Amos as an attack on the wealthy or a call for class warfare is not only superficial, but wrong and perverse: It is turning God's message of compassion into a sermon of hatred. The emphasis in Amos is on a refusal to abide by God's covenant, and a consequent tendency of the powerful to lord it over the weak. The covenant of creation and the cultural mandate gives man the opportunity to take dominion over the earth—but sinful man abuses freedom.

The lesson of Amos for Christians today is sobering: God's covenant gives us the opportunity to become His people—in reality His "priests" bearing witness to His eternal covenant of truth and righteousness. But too often we simply think and act according to the spirit of the age. If we follow our own inclinations we are likely to create oppression, sometimes in the name of fighting oppression. Only by understanding God's requirements and covenantal mercy toward us can we look at evil squarely and thus see the need for a change of mind and direction. As justice and peace come about, they will stand as a token of the coming kingdom.

THREE

THE CONTROLLED ECONOMY
Gunnar Myrdal's Subjective Conclusions
Herbert Schlossberg

Some Christians argue that a free enterprise economy harms the poor, and that government-directed economy is needed. Christians generally have not been the leaders in developing theories of directed economy, but have relied on non-Christian economists and social philosophers. Gunnar Myrdal, a Swedish economist born in 1898, has been one of the most influential proponents of governmental economic power. Examining his work will take us a long way toward understanding the popularity and problems of emphasizing the role of the state in development.

First, a few words about Myrdal's background. His early work was in the field of monetary and fiscal theory, and he became widely known through his study in the 1940s of the racial situation in the United States. He became most influential through his writings, beginning in the 1950s, in the field of development economics. That work won for him the Nobel prize in economics in 1974, which he shared with F. A. von Hayek, an Austrian economist of diametrically opposed views. Long associated with the Swedish Socialists, Myrdal was Minister of Commerce during the period 1945-47.[1]

Myrdal sees himself as an Enlightenment man. He argues that the intellectual revolution of the eighteenth century created what is best in the modern world, and calls the change from old, pre-Enlightenment values to new ones the "Great Awakening."[2] Myrdal's other ideas appear as children of the Enlightenment ideal. Thus he regards utopia not as a delusion fostered by fanatics, but as "a real goal . . . inherent in those ideas of liberty, equality, and brotherhood that are the ultimate driving forces behind the development of the modern, democratic welfare state."[3] He sees modernization ideals as an " 'official creed,' almost a national religion,"[4] and he regards modernization as impossible without central planning.[5] For this reason, Myrdal acknowledges that the value judgment that "embraces all" in his most important work on development, *Asian Drama*, is "the quest for state planning."[6]

The ends toward which Myrdal's planning process is to lead are the standard appeals of European liberalism— up to a point. Liberty and equality are the lodestones toward which the planner is drawn.[7] In the preface to *Asian Drama*, Myrdal even identifies the "American Creed" as the source of his values, with the United States being one of his two "spiritual fatherlands."[8] Yet, the components of this dual emphasis on both liberty and equality, no matter what its allegedly venerable credentials, cannot easily be reconciled. Political debates in the West for two centuries have concerned the natural tension between the two. The most forcefully expressed ideals for eradicating inequalities repeatedly have come at the expense of liberty, and Myrdal also wants to make that sacrifice. Political democracy is a fine ideal, he says, but is not to be given much weight in the quest for modernization.[9] Myrdal occasionally tries to sweeten the inevitably authoritarian cast of his recommendations, but in practice liberty has virtually no role in his movement toward utopia.

Myrdal buttresses his abandonment of the ideal of liberty by pointing out that the West already has abandoned it, with Scandinavia leading the way. The welfare state started as a bottoms-up movement and then moved gradually toward centralization and professionalism, leaving behind popular participation. Thus in the West, freedom was no more than a "liberal interlude" between mercantilism and the modern welfare state. By the same token, the capitalist and Communist worlds are moving closer together in political structures.[10] Myrdal's study of the economies of South Asia concludes that it is impossible to have a functioning democracy "without first effecting social and economic revolution."[11] In the short run decentralization, like universal suffrage, "works mostly for reaction and stagnation."[12]

MYRDAL'S SUBJECTIVISM

To understand the conclusions that Myrdal reaches, it is important to understand not only his Enlightenment base but his opposition to the positivist strain which has been so common in the social sciences, especially in the English-speaking countries. Far from denying that his values affect his science, he strongly affirms that *everyone's* science is affected by his values—especially in the social sciences. In Myrdal's thought there is no ultimate bar of truth beyond the judgment to be made by this or that society. One scholar recently concluded that in this, Myrdal was following Swedish philosopher Axel Hagerstrom's belief that value has no connection with ultimacy; value is purely individual, with no possibility of outside verification or falsification.[13]

Even in his more concrete works, Myrdal keeps returning to the same theme. "What constitutes reality," he says, "is determined by how we arrange experience."[14] This subjectivism is clear in Myrdal's use of the word *valuation* rather than *value*. He believes that "value" is used too loosely, and when he uses "valuation" he considers it to be the same as "attitude." He claims to be using the term much in the way John Dewey and other modern philosophers have done.[15] One scholar has seen in that propensity the source of Myrdal's hostility toward metaphysics of any kind; Myrdal will not acknowledge that a worldview can be rooted in anything beyond the subjective.[16]

Given Myrdal's insistence that subjectivity is inescapable, it is somewhat surprising to discover that he repeatedly calls for the elimination of bias. In a Prologue to *Asian Drama* entitled "The Beam in our Eyes," Myrdal describes the beam as the mass of preconceptions that color our questions and our conclusions—his own included. The way to eliminate bias, Myrdal says, is to make our values explicit, and nobody can fault him for not following his own advice. In a way that Myrdal does not explain, he assumes that by making our values explicit, we escape our biases and are then free to go on a crusade. Economists may be scientists, but they are also "a fighting church with a message. . . ." In fact they are "the cavalry of the social scientists."[17] Should "scientific" colleagues take him to task for this ideological purpose, he replies that they do the same thing without realizing it, being "naively innocent of their own social determinants."[18]

Myrdal sees economics as a lever that enables him to reach into and change other aspects of the society. We begin, that is, by considering economic matters, and then come to see that changes in almost every other area are also desirable—health, social stratification, social mobility, local community organization, to cite a few examples that Myrdal mentions. In his thinking the whole society is closely allied to purely economic concerns, and thus is a fit object for control. If we can plan for economic progress, we can plan for everything else. "In this way *planning becomes the intellectual matrix of the entire modernization ideology.*"[19] There is in this conception no *theoretical* limit to the scope of the planners and their agents.

Despite Myrdal's great faith in planning, he provides considerable ammunition for those who do not share it. He acknowledges that those who control social systems often remove incentives to produce and also prop themselves up against personal challenges to their authority.[20] He admits that the system of rewards prevalent in the governments of poor countries means that *"most officials have to devote most of their time and energy to limiting or stopping enterprise."*[21] But Myrdal does not go on from there to advocate the freeing of enterprise; instead, he thinks the answer to the difficulty lies in more efficient state planning.

Myrdal, a self-consciously *institutional* analyst, also disagrees with the approach of stressing "investment in man" as a strategy for inducing development. Because he insists on the primacy of institutions in effecting social change, he is naturally suspicious of relying overly on the actions and capacities of the individual.[22] There is a significant tension, to put it delicately, between Myrdal's oft-stated complaints about the effects of bad attitudes on the one hand and the determinism of his constant refusal to recognize adequately individual traits as determinants of economic performance in comparison to those relating to institutions.

On the question of the nature of historical change, Myrdal's work not only shows a similar subjectivism, but a lack of systematic focus as well. On the one hand, he believes that history comes from chance events, so there can be no such thing as historical necessity.[23] On the other hand, Myrdal sometimes finds it advantageous to speak of historical inevitabilities. Those who oppose the welfare state are tied in with "historical forces which in the long run are bound to lose out."[24] And underlying Myrdal's assumptions about the direction of history is his conviction, retained long after most of his contemporaries had abandoned it, that "belief in progress [is] the very spirit of our civilization."[25]

More interesting than those general views are Myrdal's convictions about the actual mechanisms that bring about historical change. True to his identification with the Enlightenment, he speaks about the *mechanisms* of social change.[26] The dramatic motif in *Asian Drama* comes from the conflict that Myrdal found in his subject. He says this dominated his thinking to begin with and was carried through to the end of the project. He finds dialectical tension throughout the entire fabric of life, economic, social and political. "This drama has its unity in a set of inner conflicts."[27] Although Myrdal professes no allegiance to Marxism, this Marxist idea nevertheless is obviously formative for him.

MYRDAL'S INCONSISTENCIES

How do the various elements in the society interact to bring about change? There is no clear answer to that in Myrdal's work. While he admits that education can be a key determinant of social change,[28] he also can be crassly materialistic about causation, even arguing that the lapse of a society into illiteracy could be caused by a lack of paper![29] In contrast to Myrdal's consciously "humanistic" position, his ideas are also shot through with naturalism, although that often remains deeply buried. He is always eager to promote an activist role for government and planners, and quick to interpret opposition to that orientation as excessively passive. Thus, economic conditions "need not remain as they are or evolve under the influence merely of 'natural forces.' " Students of the subject are ready to conclude, he goes on, "that very little takes care of itself in most of the countries in the region."[30] In this analysis, either the state intervenes or things must be left to natural forces. There is no room in this dichotomy for free human beings acting in ways consistent with their view of the situation and their interests and values; his conception is completely deterministic.

Like other naturalist thinkers, Myrdal has to account for the presence of evil, assuming, as he does, that human nature is fundamentally good. He consciously stands for the Enlightenment tradition that calls ideas about our sinful nature superstitious. Human beings are good and can change their own attitudes.[31] Still, he finds continually that politicians cause problems because of their incompetence and their venality. Myrdal reconciles that with his rejection of original sin by insisting that the social scientist has to examine the "mechanism of causation" that explains the politician's lapses. That mechanism is "the inherited social stratification. . . ."[32] By the same token, bad attitudes are caused by poverty.[33] With the attitudes of both the politician and the poor person caused by external circumstances rather than by personal orientation or values chosen by volition, it is clear that the human person has become something of an automaton in Myrdal's thinking.

Yet Myrdal is not consistent on that issue, and it almost seems at times as if Christians might have some points of contact with his perspective. For example, he departs from much social science thinking by stressing that human motivation is important, and that analyzing social issues without considering the volitional is unrealistic. Thus, Myrdal sees changes in attitude toward work at the heart of the problem of poverty and development. He notes that in poor countries many people do not work, and that it is their preference to be unemployed. They do not work because it is prestigious not to do so. Educated people dislike manual work especially, and when they do work they are not interested in the kind of jobs that help the economy; for them degrees are passports to sitting in government offices, which is much more prestigious than commercial and agricultural activities.

Myrdal notes that in poor countries there may be an absence of materialism in the Western sense, but that is balanced by the fact that leisure is a higher good than labor. Even when people seem busy, there is a general willingness not to accomplish a great deal. Throughout these expositions of the attitude toward work Myrdal's exasperation often breaks through the scholarship; in one place he declares it would take a miracle to get South Asians to work.[34] Although work is the example Myrdal uses most, he also speaks of other cultural determinants that are important to economic life. Some of these are the ban on the killing of cows;[35] the lack of hygiene, mostly—this is surprising to a Westerner—in the *upper* classes;[36] the lack of capacity for rational calculation among the lower classes especially.[37]

Myrdal combines his emphasis on the personal with an almost unconscious admiration for Christian virtues—unconscious in that he does not realize the theological source of those virtues. He once expressed admiration for the "Christian neighborliness" of the United States that he found absent in Europe.[38] Myrdal's list of the desirable character traits that social revolution should instill in the "new man" resembles the Protestant ethic; in essence, he wants to create a bunch of Calvinists in the Third World—without the inconvenient theology which is, in truth, all that makes Calvinists what they are.[39]

One problem, however, is that Myrdal brings to this major work on foreign cultures a faulty knowledge of his own culture. He characterizes South Asian culture in the twentieth century as equivalent to European culture in the sixteenth. His reasoning relates principally to similarities in social stratification and the lack of rationalism.[40] But that repeats Enlightenment stereotypes of the supposed intellectual stagnation that preceded the eighteenth-century secularization; it also discounts the very real economic dynamism that Europe displayed beginning in the eleventh century.

A deeper problem is that Myrdal's emphasis on culture is nullified by other observations; it is almost as if he were of two minds on the question and cannot decide. The "institutional" approach which he continuously and self-consciously advocates is itself at least a check on emphasizing cultural matters. For example, Myrdal believes the caste system is an economic disaster, besides its moral defects, and that it became worse after independence than before. But he also believes that "political processes" caused the difficulty and only by reforming *them* can the caste system be derailed.[41] Thus the cultural reality is caused by an institutional process, rather than the other way around. It is not cultural change that will effect economic performance, but politics—providing it's the right kind of politics. Similarly, he debunks the repeated calls for an intellectual and moral conversion as the answer to India's problems, insisting that this is hopeless, unless the social institutions are changed. And the way to do this is through political action.[42]

Myrdal thus grasps cultural explanations, but his ideology wars against them. He does not want explanations of economic stagnation to include tales of natives enjoying their preference for leisure, and judges that racism is partly to blame for such stories. He thinks such reasoning is condescending and demeaning, but his basic objection is apparently that it is defeatist. For if economic failure is a function of such unpromising candidates for social manipulation as culturally derived preferences, there is no point in discussing measures to be taken.[43]

MYRDAL'S FAITH

Much to be preferred, for Myrdal, is the manipulation of the culture by the planner. When the requisite "social revolution" has been effected, there will be formed a "national community" in which "the barriers of caste, color, religion, ethnic origin, culture, language, and provincial loyalties would be broken down. . . ."[44] The hold of tradition on villagers will have to be broken; in fact the village itself will have to disappear, as Western experts have been advocating.[45] Myrdal's analysis of the labor supply in poor countries also emphasizes the role of the planner. The supply is actually smaller than the typical demographic statistics suggest because they do not take into consideration the poor attitudes that derogate from the supply of useful labor. Myrdal's planner, however, compensates for that by changing those attitudes by means of "education, propaganda, leadership, regulations, and compulsion." In that way, "The magnitude of the labor reserve is a function of the policy measures assumed to be applied." This makes the labor reserve dynamic rather than static. The planner breaks the status quo. Under this conception, labor supply equals the existing labor reserve plus the effects of the planner's initiatives.[46] Myrdal's discussion of education has the same instrumental quality. The attitudes of the population must be changed, and this change must be accomplished by means of "punishments and inducements" to be incorporated in legislation, both of which he considers to be parts of the *educational* process.[47]

Myrdal's examination of culture does not omit religion. Good Enlightenment man that he is, he thinks that taking religion seriously is not a Western trait, and is nothing more than superstition. He believes that these irrational conceptions "have not commonly been held in the West for centuries."[48] This is a serious failure in his understanding of the intellectual history of his own culture and sets the stage for errors in his understanding of development. At the same time, Myrdal argues that religion, understood rightly, need not conflict with the modernization ideals; as long as religion is "relegated to private life, it should not influence those in public life."[49] But of course, it is those "private" attitudes that have done so much damage to economic life in poor countries. Thus what Myrdal is calling for is not only a privatized religion, but one that is completely irrelevant even to the private aspects of individual and family life.[50]

Planners, according to Myrdal, should have authority over religion, as they should have authority over all determinants of social behavior. Religion can even become another tool in the planner's kit, as he conveys socially useful ideas packaged in religious language. This makes sense to Myrdal because for him the dogmas are nonsense; the accidents are for him the essence, and that means they are only "a ritualized and stratified complex of highly emotional beliefs and valuations that give the sanction of sacredness, taboo and immutability to inherited institutional arrangements, modes of living, and attitudes."[51] Hence the emphasis on education as a means of social control: Let the peasants keep their rituals as long as they serve to validate and transmit the planner's conception of what is socially useful.

Myrdal, in short, wants a godlike planning elite. He praises "democracy" but frankly argues that people must not be permitted to do as they wish. In the underdeveloped countries, Myrdal notes, people hold values that are not compatible with those he believes are necessary for development. The only solution is for the planners either to overrule or to circumvent popular opinion. The elite are thus "the active *subject*" and the masses are "the relatively passive *objects*" of the plan.[52]

To Myrdal, the enemy is complacency, and the people must be roused from their lethargy.[53] The self-proclaimed Enlightenment philosopher is especially glad about the role of the elite in India because it has fostered "enlightened" ideas of modernization.[54] In spite of his recognition that no workable plan seems to emerge from the elite, Myrdal still favors their domination because the planning ideology "serves as a rationalization for interventionist practices."[55] The domination of the elite, regardless of their failures, is essential, because only the elite have the possibility of freeing man from the environmentalist web.

It is remarkable that Myrdal argues all of this despite his conviction that values are entirely subjective, a position which undercuts any justification for forcing his beliefs on other people.[56] He argues out of faith in the control of an elite which will not rule capriciously, but in relation to a plan. For Myrdal, central planning that can save Third-World economies has this meaning:

> The basic principle in the ideology of economic planning is that the state shall take an active, indeed the decisive, role in the economy: by its own acts of investment and enterprise, and by its various controls—inducements

and restrictions—over the private sector, the state shall initiate, spur, and steer economic development. These public policy measures shall be rationally coordinated, and the coordination be made explicit in an over-all plan for a specified number of years ahead.[57]

One justification Myrdal uses for this model in poor countries is his conviction that it made the difference in those that are now rich—much more than is generally acknowledged. It is the only means available for poor countries to break out of their stagnation, he contends.[58] Although a common criticism of centralized economies is their rigidity and stagnation, Myrdal argues that central planning is the way to add flexibility and productivity to the economy.[59] Evidently the reason for this is his view that the poor countries are dominated by hidebound traditions, and that the external force of government decrees are necessary to break their power. Oddly enough, he thought in the late sixties that this view was universally accepted, that the need for central planning was almost beyond dispute.[60]

How are we to understand what central planning should accomplish? Myrdal uses a vehicular metaphor; the government engages itself in "steering the economy."[61] While the state steers the economy it also regulates the throttle, since it must concern itself with the pace of expansion.[62] This imagery invites us to think of the planner as firmly in control of the situation, but Myrdal's thinking is ambiguous on this point. He also sees the planner as engaged in the process of "negotiation," playing off various interests against each other. The lower administrative and political divisions retain "a measure of autonomy." Along with this, of course, the central government holds "the levers of control."[63]

Other ambivalences dot Myrdal's work. He prefers private financing to public because it includes the "taboo" that loans must be repaid; that requirement produces a certain discipline. Without that discipline, international finance is left to politics "where the crackpots and demagogues swim with great pleasure."[64] He distrusts not only politicians but also administrators, and he wants their discretion to be cut to a minimum.[65]

How can Myrdal recommend central planning when he knows that the power corrupts both the planner and the one who implements the plan? His work is full of the anguish of one who advocates utopia with all his being while at the same time retaining the necessary honesty to record the failures of utopia. He finds it paradoxical that even when planning is successful, "inequalities have generally not decreased since independence." If anything, Myrdal observes, they have increased in all the countries of South Asia, with the possible exception of Ceylon. He finds the reason to be stated accurately in a report of the Indian government: the increase of central control provided the opportunity for special interests to capture the government; in this way the middle and upper classes use the whole process for their own benefit. Thus he regards the political forces with utter contempt. "The stakes the politicians play for are not opportunities to advance the national interest but power, prestige, personal advantage, patronage, and graft."[66]

If planning and centralization are so devastating, why isn't the laissez-faire economy a good alternative? The reason is Myrdal's conviction, often expressed, that it cannot allow for economic development. When he talks about laissez-faire policies practiced by the British in India, he says that they led to "the impoverishment of indigenous economic enterprise."[67] It is only three hundred pages later that we learn that this exercise in "laissez-faire" included the characteristic that when cash crops led to increased incomes, that increase was promptly taken away by a tax increase imposed by the British government.[68] Thus, there is some question of what he means by "laissez-faire."

MYRDAL'S OTHER BLIND SPOTS

Myrdal's analysis of foreign aid is also full of contradictions. An emphasis on the importance of capital is for Myrdal as well as for most mainstream development economists the main justification of the need for foreign aid. Myrdal sees that foreign investors tended to steer clear of South Asian governments. He notes that there are "cumbersome controls" and an uncongenial political environment. Yet, Myrdal often seems oblivious to the connection between those conditions and the reluctance of foreign investors to invest.[69] He frankly notes that, in comparison with private capital, foreign aid has a very short time horizon. That is one reason so much is misallocated. In view of his bias toward central planning, it's surprising to read Myrdal's frank assessment that the public money entering the region is "doubtless inferior in quality" to the private capital it replaced.[70] And yet, he still calls for greater governmental foreign aid.

Some of the most perplexing features of Myrdal's writings on economic development involve his claim of reverence for democracy and liberty. Throughout *Asian Drama*

Myrdal severely criticizes the regimes of South Asia, none of which can be considered liberal in the classical sense, for being *soft states*, a term so characteristic of the work that it has come to be associated with his name. In contrast to that "softness," he repeatedly calls for the state to direct the efforts of its citizens: "[C]ompulsion plays a strategic role." Its absence is part of a "masquerade."[71] Even the most authoritarian regimes in the region are too soft for him. They have a preference for the Western model over the Eastern, but that approach is too slow; they cannot step up the pace of modernization without the willingness to intervene more forcefully in the social fabric.[72] He reaches the same conclusion Machiavelli did in *The Prince*: It is easier and preferable to impose big changes rapidly, rather than small changes incrementally. "But institutions can ordinarily be changed only by resort to what in the region is called compulsion—putting obligations on people and support them by force." This is followed by criticisms of those who are influenced by the West to take the gradualist approach.[73]

Yet Myrdal acknowledges also that far from being "western" with respect to compulsion, the regimes in South Asia already use more administrative discretion than in the West and more than the West at a comparable stage of development.[74] Still more compulsion, evidently, is needed. The main cultural trait that has to be broken is the lack of social discipline, and compulsion is his way of accomplishing that feat. He regards this trait as the main difference between the West and Asia at comparable points in their development. His belief in the importance of discipline is so strong that he is distressed that the various planning documents in South Asia do not mention it.[75] When the planners do their work well they do it comprehensively. They work in "all fields of social and economic life."[76]

Since culture is a crucial element in economic life for Myrdal, it is consistent that he wants the cultural life of the society also brought under the planner's control. In the government's drive to change attitudes, the schools are the obvious tools. The ultimate criterion for what is to be taught must be the development ideology. Moreover, the concept of "education" is expanded to include punishments and other inducements designed to change attitudes. It follows from this that such private education that remains free from government control—not much that is formally private actually retains that freedom—is disruptive to the planner's purposes and must be curtailed.[77]

The main issue for Myrdal, as for anyone who wishes to invest political authorities with a plenitude of power, has to be, "What use is actually made by political authorities when they are given that power?" Myrdal's answer is surprisingly gloomy, given his prescriptions. As soon as the planning process is begun the businessmen show up to participate in it, including those from abroad. That is because the effect of planning is "to create vested interests," among which the planners must choose. This makes *lobbying* one of the most important of entrepreneurial functions. Even Socialist countries follow the same process. As a result,

> these controls mostly work in favor of established business, and particularly big business. . . . Against this background it becomes more understandable why businessmen and other inherently conservative strata do not

offer more opposition to equalization, socialism, and the plethora of direct and discriminatory controls. . . .[78]

That explains why, in spite of an army of officials supposedly looking out for the poor, it is the rich who benefit. It seems to make little difference whether the system is formally democratic or not, or whether it is capitalist or Socialist.[79]

In South Asia, Myrdal believes, there is no such thing as private business in the Western sense. Businessmen favor the kind of controls that Myrdal finds disadvantageous—*discretionary controls*, which are dependent on the ad hoc decisions of officials. Under those conditions, administrators determine who gets government services, loans, foreign exchange and other benefits. The frustration level for businessmen is very high in a system like that, but the opportunities to amass riches are even higher. "All this tends to restrict competition, favor monopoly and oligopoly, and pamper vested interests."[80] In India the highly touted community action programs turned out to be a way for the rich to get more subsidies. The easy credit program which was supposed to bypass the moneylenders became the means for moneylenders to get cheap money.[81] Even when particular private interests are not served by the administrative structure, sectional interests are. That explains why the price controls on agricultural products invariably favor urban populations, while taking the livelihood from the peasantry.[82]

The upshot of such a situation is perfectly predictable: corruption is endemic throughout the poor countries. The politicians go through the motions of cleaning house from time to time, but the condition exists at all levels of the government. It spreads to the minor officials as a natural consequence of its presence among the powerful. The foreign firms that must conduct their affairs in such an environment regard the bribes as a cost of business which they pay willingly. Myrdal introduces an irony into this discussion: it is difficult to establish free markets for business activities in South Asia, but it has been done in the public sector, just the opposite of what happens in the West. This is a market in bribes rather than in products and services that the public desires. Because of all this, Myrdal says, irrationality and uncertainty are introduced into the plan.[83]

In sum, Myrdal's theory holds that the political process must be elevated to the dominant position if the poor countries are to leave the wilderness of poverty. But in the actual event, "most officials have to devote most of their time and energy to limiting or stopping enterprise."[84] The evident candor in these damaging admissions would be more admirable if Myrdal would recognize that these conditions are inherent in the system he champions but not in the one he opposes.

CONCLUSIONS

What can we say about such an intellectual morass? It would be easy to say merely that Myrdal is confused, but it is worse than that: Myrdal's views have been disastrous for the countries that have tried them. Here are some of the weaknesses in Myrdal's approach to development economics.

—*Myrdal, the Nobel laureate in economics, refuses to use the tools of economics in testing his ideas.* He refuses to admit that price is in any way normative in establishing the relationship between supply and demand, and instead calls for "price policies."[85] This is tantamount to discrediting the messenger in advance of even learning what the message is. He once told an interviewer that shareholders play no economic role and also that Milton Friedman threatens the world like atom bombs.[86] That may be to some extent the testiness of an old man whose life's work is being repudiated by the course of events, but it also comports well with his propensity, going back decades, for giving more credence to his ideology (or, as he puts it, his *valuations*) than to either factual or theoretical considerations.

—*Myrdal has a wrong doctrine of human nature.* His constant harping on the environment as the determinant of behavior is solidly rooted in his ideological commitment. The Enlightenment, he says, rid us of the "superstition" that evil was rooted in human character, although the older view is still all too commonly held. He believes the Enlightenment conclusion has been confirmed by social science research. Yet, since man is "good," he can "change his attitudes."[87] This is a startling contradiction, which Myrdal thinks he resolves by positing that the optimistic view is true on one level and the pessimistic one on the other. But this is plainly a mystification that absolves him from the need to reconcile the dark picture that accompanies his determinism with the bright picture that is tied to his value of freedom. He does not recognize that value as a remnant from the Christian faith he has discarded.

—*Myrdal's system shows an absence of justice.* The intense pragmatism, the lack of principle in Myrdal's thinking shows up in many ways. As the planner "negotiates" with the various actors in the political structure, he plays them against one another. Having adopted the Enlightenment ethic, in which transcendent ethical principles were dissolved, Myrdal has no principle which can show one course of action to be just and another unjust.

After his active career had drawn to a close, Myrdal looked back on it and concluded that he had been a rebel.[88] Yet in a broader sense Myrdal has been very much a man of his times, as we might expect of someone who calls himself an Enlightenment philosopher. He is at one with the spirit of the age, and especially with the social sciences, in his rejection of God's law and its relevance to the realities of social life; in his pragmatism; in the contradictions between his humanitarian ethic and its lack of any metaphysical foundation; in the despair he has expressed often in recent years: "Now we see that the world is going to hell, now that we're going to die."[89]

The Enlightenment mindset has been at the heart of most of Myrdal's failure of vision. It explains why he could call so persistently for the consideration of cultural factors, while ignoring or undervaluing religion and the other values that men hold most deeply. The materialism of Enlightenment anthropology has no real place for culture. Nor has it any place for freedom. Hence, with the evident sincerity of his respect for liberty and the principles of the American republic, he nevertheless advocates a politically-driven economy that destroys liberty. Hating the oppression and venality of the corruption that is endemic in poor countries, Myrdal is the apologist for economies in which economic favors are in the hands of politicians and bureaucrats, thus making corruption inevitable.

Myrdal is the exemplar of so much that is wrong with modern government planning in order to help the poor. Rooted in assumptions that depart from the Biblical underpinnings of our civilization, Myrdal's ideas carry over the moral fervor but none of the understandings that are necessary for bringing healthy vibrant economies into existence. Yet, so ingrained is Enlightenment thinking in our academic elite that Myrdal has been suggested for a Nobel Peace Prize.[90] That his wobbly thinking has received such praise is a clear indication that anti-Biblical economic thought has come to a dead end.

THE PURSUIT OF UTOPIA

Clark H. Pinnock

*W*e live in an era of the unprecedented expansion of the Christian movement throughout the world. Ours is a hopeful time of great opportunity for discipling the nations and making a significant impact upon cultures around the world, particularly in the direction of relief and development. Disagreement accompanies that opportunity, though. Christians disagree on how believers should pursue the task of helping the poor, aside from acts of generous charity, on which we generally do not disagree. Ideology is dividing Christians from one another: In our search for answers to the problem of poverty some look to socialism and its constellation of ideas, while others have different recommendations.

It would be pleasant to leave ideology aside and concentrate entirely upon "kingdom" issues, but that, sadly, is not possible. An ideology is basically a set of ideas which attempts to explain the world and suggests ways to change it for the better; an ideology can also trap and seduce us by blinding the mind and preventing it from seeing reality.[1] Just as Amos criticized heatedly the popular ungodliness of his time, so we cannot discuss ways for Christians to help the poor without, to some extent, attacking an ideology that is leading many people astray. The fashionable theory in Amos' time we might call Jereboamism; the fashionable theory among many Christians now is heavily influenced by Marxism.

To be blunt, I am troubled at the way in which our proper Christian concern for the poor has been unwisely routed along the tracks of collectivist economics. That long detour seriously jeopardizes the possibility of doing effective good and threatens to short-circuit well-meaning Christian intentions. If we are serious about "God's preferential option for the poor" (to use the jargon of liberation theology), then it is neither wise nor prudent to side with an ideology which, as I will argue, has such a bad record in regard to reducing the misery of poor people. This essay will examine the issue of ideological entrapment in relationship to the fashionable utopian fallacy of our time, and then discuss the betrayal of the poor by those who have embraced the fallacy.

A SAD CASE OF IDEOLOGICAL ENTRAPMENT

My argument is that our frequent lack of good judgment about poverty questions is rooted in an entrapment. Whenever the issue of ideological entrapment is raised, some believers cite the Nazi "Christians" (or perhaps, to some, even the religious right in the United States) as examples of a bad tendency. But there is a very serious case of entrapment which few are willing to name: the tendency of a significant number of church leaders in the twentieth century to tie the cause of God's kingdom to the cause of communism, or socialism in some milder form.

This entangling alliance can be compared without

much exaggeration to the alignment in Germany of the kingdom of God with the Nazi ideology.[2] What makes the comparison appropriate is the fact that the Marxist movement is not just a failure as a self-proclaimed revolutionary force in improving the lot of the poor, but is also a unique historical evil even in the twentieth century, which has witnessed many evils on a massive scale. Marxism has led to the starvation and murder of millions of victims on the very borders of the West, while many of our political and intellectual leaders and even some church leaders have looked the other way and prattled on about the bright new hope of socialism. Alexander Solzhenitsyn and many others have documented the torture and oppression carried out by Socialist dictators against their own unfortunate peoples. Between fascism and communism there seems to be no practical difference.[3]

There is a danger of getting sidetracked into telling the dismal story of the romance of certain churchmen with Marxism and the left in general; what we really need to focus on is the foolish act of endorsing collectivist economic practice which has harmed the poor so much. But just as Amos had to put the deviations of his time in historical perspective, so we can only understand the attraction of Socialist theories concerning poverty by placing them in the context of the broader entrapment. We have to see that socialism is the great political myth of the twentieth century, and that its appeal is precisely mythical and not empirical. No one could be attracted to socialism on empirical grounds because evidence of its successes does not exist. The attraction is the seductive appeal which myth has for the human imagination.[4]

Briefly, then, let's itemize some of the pieces of evidence which reveal ideological entrapment. Before 1960 support for Marxism was visible in what Paul Hollander calls political tourism.[5] Hewlett Johnson (the pathetic and amusing Red Dean of Canterbury), along with many intellectuals such as Bernard Shaw, Arthur Koestler, and Malcolm Muggeridge, traveled to the Soviet Union in the thirties, at the very time when Stalin was consolidating his total power and beginning to liquidate millions under his iron rule. They came back to the West singing the praises of the great Socialist revolution in Russia. Their desire to believe the seductive promises of the revolutionary myth robbed them of practically every vestige of critical reason.[6]

Since 1960 the situation has actually deteriorated further. Christians on the left no longer praise Stalin, but some continue to applaud the ideology on which he based his murderous power. So-called liberation theologians and church leaders proclaim an alliance between Christians and Marxists and see socialism as the way to move beyond class-based society.[7] Miranda, admittedly more radical than most, goes so far as to equate communism and Christianity.[8] True, the various liberationist writers usually take pains to say they find fault with some dimensions of Marxism, but their criticisms are never so radical as to prevent them from supporting Marxist revolutions. In their view, no matter what is wrong with socialism, capitalism is worse. In line with this thinking the World Council of Churches has assisted Marxist guerrillas in Africa under the guise of combating racism. In a brilliant display of double standards, these same churchmen are silent about human rights violations in Cuba, Ethiopia, and Angola while complaining bitterly about infractions in South Africa and El Salvador.

Political pilgrims are currently flocking to Nicaragua to see the latest revolution firsthand.[9]

Some Christians support a very ugly reality in a less direct way. The sainted "peace movement," for example, is supported by many who have good intentions but little prudence. Those who forget the failure of Neville Chamberlain's attempts to appease Hitler are intent upon reducing our military preparedness in the face of a Soviet Union bursting with missiles and tanks but little else. The peace movement's greatest success so far was to compel a U.S. retreat from Vietnam and help to make possible the genocide in Cambodia and the wretched oppression of Communist Vietnam from which thousands continue to try to flee in flimsy boats upon dangerous seas. Yet some Christians do not seem to recognize how their noble-sounding efforts serve the cause of Marxist oppression. It feels so good to be for "peace" that they do not want to spoil it by facing facts. The slogans differ, but they are as unrealistically optimistic about international developments as their counterparts were in Amos' day.

Sadly, many contemporary churchmen seem to accept double standards and speak out only on behalf of politically approved victims. The silence that greets even the cries of Christian believers under communism is one example of this.[10] Jews are noted for speaking out about the oppression of their fellow religionists, but few Christians say anything about the persecution of believers under communism. It was terribly sad when even Billy Graham, visiting the U.S.S.R. in 1982, professed to notice no evidence of religious repression in the Soviet Union, and then virtually endorsed the "peace" concerns of the Soviet state himself.

Evidently he did not press hard for information about fellow Baptists in prison, perhaps for fear of lessening his chances to return in the future.

More folly is evident when many churchmen enthusiastically endorse Lenin's discredited theory that poverty in the two-thirds world was somehow caused by the prosperity of the West. Lenin concocted that dependency theory to explain why Marx's own predictions about capitalism had failed so badly, and to account for the rising standard of living on the part of the proletariat in the West. Lenin's gambit obviously has great appeal for the leaders of impoverished states looking for someone to blame for their own deficiencies or bad decisions, but its appeal for Western churchmen can only be explained in terms of seduction by Marxist myth. In actuality, rich countries mostly trade among themselves, and other countries are prosperous in direct proportion to their contact with the West. The poorest places are those with little or no contact.[11]

Even in my own country of Canada the same pattern of ritual condemnation for politically and economically liberal societies is evident. We are told, for example, that although we suppose ourselves to be living in an open society with reasonable opportunities for all, in actual fact we really suffer from an oppressive class structure and need a Socialist order to be installed in its place.[12]

Overall, there is little difference in some Christian reaction to the two movements, fascism and communism, at moments when each has seemed to be the wave of the future. Many churchmen are now supporting the Marxist ideology in one version or another in much the same way as others had supported the Nazi ideology in the Third Reich. Won't people in a hundred years' time look back in amazement at the way in which Christian leaders became accomplices of both really vicious political movements?

There is even a distinct possibility that support from churchmen, coming at a time when Marxism has lost most of its legitimacy and mythical appeal, owing to its brutality and colossal failures, will actually prolong the life of Communist empires. What a supreme irony it would be if Christians were to give Marxism the religious legitimacy which it could never have generated for itself as a secular doctrine!

THE UTOPIAN FALLACY

The alignment of some Christians with Marxism can be explained by invoking the category of the utopian myth. Human hope for salvation in history—the millennial longing for a world purified of evil—is immense. Christianity provides a solution, but those who want change according to their timetable, not God's, sweep aside even developed criticial judgment in their rush to force open the gates of Eden. In this respect socialism possesses a clear "advantage" over capitalism. Socialism is one of the most powerful myths of the modern era, and the fact that it is nowhere realized only adds to its appeal.

It is vital to understand that a fugitive vision of this sort forever tantalizes those who long for it. Capitalism may produce better results in terms of productivity. It may produce a better car at a cheaper price. Capitalism, however, cannot compete with socialism in the area of romantic appeal.[13] This quality of romance has enabled Marxists to disregard the empirical data and persist in policies long after they have been seen to be ruinous. Western intellectuals and weary churchmen in particular can become fixated on utopia. Many have lost confidence in God, but have not given up on God's millennium; so they become sheep following a worldly ideology that promises to achieve it for them. Perhaps, they now begin to hope, man can through reason bring the ideal world about on his own without having to call on God. Marx is the prophet of such a humanist vision.

Putting a utopian vision into practice does little harm if the people involved participate voluntarily in the experiment and always have the right to opt out. The historical record shows, however, that those who try to create a utopia in a fallen world always end up using force and coercion to require people to do what the vision dictates is right. They introduce terror and soon find out that only terror is left. This is the lesson of the coercive utopias of Marxism. And this is the reason why we find ourselves dealing not only with failed economics but finally with murder and genocide as well.

Understandably, given our theology, Christians may be particularly vulnerable to ideological seduction from the utopian left. For one thing, God's Spirit makes us sensitive to our own sins and failings, and this can alienate us from our own admittedly imperfect society. Indeed some of us feel so keenly the shortcomings of Western culture that we are prone to accept even false charges hurled against it and idealize societies just out of view, especially if they make a claim to social justice as Marxist regimes always do.

Paradoxically, it is easy for us to become estranged from our own society at the very moment when millions are desperate to emigrate to it. Somehow that Socialist utopia just over the horizon must be a better place, we think, whether it be Tanzania, South Yemen or Albania.

Just listen to the Christian terminology they use about equality and brotherhood!

But a deeper cause of our willing seduction lies in the millennial dimension of the gospel message itself. Do we not pray, "Thy kingdom come, thy will be done in earth, as it is in heaven" (Matt 6:10)? Do we not long to see Christ transform the nations and create a just and peaceful society? Of course we do, and this very fact exposes us to hucksters peddling the miracle ideology guaranteed to deliver the millennium for us. Since our theology gives us the will to believe in a better world, ideologues are more than happy to offer us satisfaction.[14] In a sense our faith sets us up to be deceived, if we are not watchful. How easy it is to be indifferent about practicalities in the realm of hope and religion, how easy to want to treat all people as if they were saints not sinners, how easy to relish a foolish course of action in the name of a greater faith!

The lesson here is that the only morally acceptable utopian is a very careful one, one who does not let his hope for a better world cause him to despise his experience of how the world actually works. Hope is an important quality which enables people to undertake heroic projects; but hope which refuses to be prudent can lead to disaster not only for ourselves, but for those who did not ask to be objects of experiment. Whatever moral grandeur can be found in the rhetoric of Marx is more than destroyed in the deadly havoc which has resulted from the implementation of his theories.

One of the great ironies of modern theology is the impact of the great rediscovery of Jesus' central category, the kingdom of God. It released a fresh impulse of political theology akin to the older post-millennial Reformed social vision into our thinking. Sadly, the rediscovery was quickly hijacked and fused with a secularized utopian vision, and then turned into a nightmare. I myself am eager to read the Bible as the story of God's liberation of the oppressed, and have found this to be a hermeneutical key able to unlock many exegetical and pastoral doors. But what a terrible shame when this Biblical hope is tied to the political fortunes and strategies of the left, to an ideology which delivers slavery, not liberation. If we want an ideology to accompany the kingdom, we ought to look for one which offers at least a glimmer of hope.

Part of today's problem also lies in the secularization of the faith of certain of the theologians themselves. I would not want to suggest that all left-leaning Christians suffer from a loss of faith. But it is clear that political theology can easily be a substitute for faith rather than an expression of it. Owing to a crisis of faith in the message of the Bible, religious liberals during the past two centuries have sought to perform various kinds of salvage operations in order to have something left over once the old faith disappeared.[15] Since it is painful to live in a world from which God has disappeared, it is natural for some to take up Marxism to fill the void, particularly since Marxism is a caricature of Christianity, offering the millennium without God.

Two additional minor elements also help to explain the remarkable attraction Marxism and the left has had for many non-Christian intellectuals and certain Christians. One has to do with social class. A new class has arisen in the developed world around the function of the production and dissemination of symbolic knowledge. "New class" people are employed in the education sector, in the communications media, in therapy and counseling, and in governmental bureaucracies; many tend to look down on the old middle class which was concerned with business. We should not overlook the power of selfishness among those who claim to be altruistic; many on the left value government subsidies on which their own salaries often depend. They have reason to expect that a centrally planned society will retain their services; they see advantages in extending its interventions into even more areas of society. This makes them natural allies of the left, and among their number, of course, are many of the professional theologians who also know which side their bread is buttered on.[16]

Furthermore, intellectuals are unlike ordinary people in that they tend to feed upon ideas rather than realities. Many like nothing better than the grand theory which seems to tie everything together in a perfect mental system. Therefore, many gravitate to utopian schemes like Marx's, and it seldom crosses their minds to ask the prosaic question of why the masses prosper under market economies and suffer deprivation under centrally planned systems. It is a failing to which intellectuals easily fall prey.

The specter of Marxism as a failed myth comes clearly to expression in the new English edition of the work of Ernst Bloch. His large work (some 1500 pages in English translation) is perhaps the most extravagant defense of Marxism ever mounted. Here we see a man whose mind was so obsessed by the hope for paradise that he refused to look reality in the face. Looking forward to the Novum, to the kingdom of God without God, he was able to persuade himself that this glorious future had begun to take shape in the Soviet system. From the purges, from the gulags, from the forced collectivization, Bloch has evidently learned nothing. The only fascism he can see is in the United States. Here we find a man so obsessed by utopia that he can condone mass murder in its name.[17]

In the end the legacy of Marx is to have bequeathed a myth to the world so strong that it can withstand a thousand refutations. Brutality and folly notwithstanding, the vision is likely to endure because of its seductive power, particularly if Christians are taken in by it.

A BETRAYAL OF THE POOR

Turning now from the broader picture to the more specific problem of poverty and its relief, let's move from theory to practice. Let's be concerned for the poor themselves, for the missed opportunities in relation to helping them, and for the harm which is done to them by means of bad public policy which feeds upon Socialist myth. In this area, good intentions are simply not enough. They can bring disaster upon the people we want to help if hopes are not informed by wisdom and prudence. Ignorance is not harmless; in the real world our illusions can have awful consequences.

In short, we must learn to look closely at practicalities, at real outcomes. It is a wicked thing, for example, to weaken a society which holds some promise to raise the poor from deprivation, and to give support to a self-styled utopia which does not. Such activity is not just an intellectual error which can be brushed aside: It inflicts real pain upon those least able to bear it. A "good" ideology, like a good bridge, carries vehicles across the valley; a "bad" ideology harms people, including the poor. The system which offers freedom and opportunity for material advancement to the poor is a good system in practice. No theology deserves to be called a "liberation" theology unless it can be shown to produce liberation from poverty. Otherwise it is a sham and a fraud.[18]

The sham has strong support among self-styled liberation theologians who link the gospel and socialism in a very exclusive way. The definite preference for socialism and keen distaste for democratic capitalism among them is obvious.[19] It might be unrealistic to expect some theologians to be proponents of market economics, but we should not tolerate absolute blindness to the failure of Marxist economics. Whatever may be the perceptions of market economics from the South American standpoint, the fact remains that Marxism has been tried and found seriously wanting. The verdict is in: Socialism is a utopian vision which in practice betrays the poor, and for this reason ought to be repudiated. Precisely for the sake of the poor, we must stop dreaming and begin to accept economic reality.[20]

It seems almost necessary to shake some churchmen and say: Don't just look, see! See how centrally planned economies fail to be productive. All the countries in the Soviet empire prove the point, as do all those unfortunate African states which have tried Marxism. China has had all the problems also, but is now adopting some market strategies that are beginning to work. The basic reason for socialism's failure also is clear. It shackles the dynamic creativity of people which is the source of wealth creation, and replaces it with a vast bureaucracy which is notoriously inefficent. Instead of serving the people at large, it serves the "nomenklatura" or the ruling class in the system.

It is important not to lose sight of this point. Socialism *does* serve a group of people very well, namely the functionaries of the state apparatus. Socialism is hard to dislodge because this large ruling class has a strong vested interest in maintaining the status quo. Significantly, the semi-Socialist welfare states of the West run on the same principle: Welfare state policies intended for the poor primarily increase the material well-being of the administering bureaucracies. The rhetoric may be social justice, but the reality is economic payoffs to the politically favored.

Marxist systems hurt most people because they make economic calculation impossible. Nothing can rival the efficiency with which the market sets prices and indicates priorities. Central economic planning simply cannot compete with the way the system of private property rights (this is what "capitalism" really is) encourages efficiency and growth. Democracy also is not possible under Marxism because neither political nor economic liberties can be tolerated if the system is to work. It is all very well to protest and say that the Soviet Union is not the "model" of socialism one wishes to follow—but wishes are not facts, and the fact of the matter is that the theory of central planning itself implies the Soviet practice or something very like it.[21]

Don't just look, see! How many more Tanzanias will we have to endure before the lesson is learned? For twenty years Julius Nyerere sought to impose upon his unfortunate country a Socialist dream, supposedly in an African mode. He carried out a brutal policy of forced resettlement against a resistant rural people. The plan has not worked; the country is deeper in poverty than before. Tanzania has been the recipient of more aid per capita than any other country, and the economy is ruined. Yet for much of this time we have heard Western churchmen praising the "Christian social order" promoted by Mr. Nyerere. When will we ever learn that socialism yields neither dignity nor freedom nor prosperity?[22] When will we accept socialism's historical record, which shows that the worst unintended consequences follow on the heels of the best intentions?

Market economies, on the other hand, have been remarkably and even spectacularly successful in raising the standard of living of whole populations. No system has ever been so effective in wealth creation and productive power.[23] That is true not only of the Western powers in general, but true also in modern Asia where Japan has in forty years become a giant economic power, where South Korea, Taiwan, Hong Kong, and Singapore are all booming economically, and where Mainland China itself is throwing Marx away in favor of market incentives. Pointing to these Asian countries is very important here because their experience proves that recently poor countries can even now raise themselves from poverty, not by opting out of but by entering into the world capitalist system.[24]

Again, it is obvious why this is happening. Liberal economies have the ability to make full use of knowledge and human creativity. In an open system, anyone can try out a new product or approach to see if it will work. If the idea is a dud, the market will blow it away just as quickly as it appeared, with very little waste of resources. But if the idea is a winner, people will vote for it when they decide to buy the product or service. There is simply no way that a centrally planned, top-down economy can perform this function in a comparable way. Socialism may sound good in theory and look good on paper, but it simply does not work. The simple truth is that wealth is more effectively generated within a market economy than a state-owned economy.[25]

To put it in different terms, the market approach works well because it is realistic about human nature. Socialism works poorly because it presupposes saints. The market puts people in a position where it is to their own advantage as well as to ours that they serve us well. The baker will try to produce a fine loaf not because he is morally good (he often is), but because we will shop elsewhere if he does not. Thus his prosperity depends on serving us well. The system requires him to perform politely and capably, whatever his mood or his morals. In this way the system makes the best of a fallen world, and operates shrewdly and well within it.

At the same time it's important to add that the exchange economy presupposes a degree of truthfulness and honesty in the making and keeping of agreements. It presumes upon a measure of moral character which it lies in the province of religion to foster. To function well, a market economy requires certain human qualities such as self-discipline, honesty, and a belief in the future. If those qualities are absent or in decline, the market system is in danger. But those traits are not utopian. They can be acquired in various ways—most completely, through Christian conversion.

A comparison of socialism and capitalism with respect to their ability to supply political liberties and material abundance shows capitalism to be the clear winner. It is far from perfect, of course, but it is the most truly revolutionary force yet discovered in relation to the realization of material well-being. Consequently, capitalism is and ought to be the natural ally for any liberation theology which is serious about liberty, political and economic.

The dynamics at work here transcend merely theoretical ideology. Again, a good mechanic is the one who can fix my brakes, and a good economic theory is the one which in application makes the best use of scarce resources and generates the most wealth for the greatest number, without doing injustice to others. For this practical reason I think it is obvious that Christians ought to give their qualified support to the practice of capitalism and the market economy. For years left-wing churchmen have sung the praises of such disastrous experiments as Ghana and Cuba. It is now time for us to give at least two cheers for capitalism. Why is it wrong to give due credit to a system which delivers freedom and prosperity, when a failed theory has been praised for decades?

Christians should speak on behalf of the market approach, because poor societies are looking for good advice and even depend upon it. Our support for capitalism has to be qualified. Our society in North America and Europe is badly flawed, partly because of the harm which material abundance does when it is selfishly consumed. The success of the market in supplying people's needs can also be their downfall morally and spiritually. Ironically, the prosperity of the West (which is due to its Christian capitalist heritage) is the very thing which Satan, the beguiling serpent, now uses to jeopardize the vitality of the churches. But at least, in a free economy, individuals have the opportunity to make stewardly use of their resources, since they have an opportunity to invest in the kingdom of God and on behalf of those in need. In Marxist economies, the opportunity is taken away.

It is important for church leaders to speak out on behalf of peace and justice. Their witness can be the inspiration and source of hope for millions of Christians. But it is also important, when ministers wish to address specific issues, that they make use of the expertise required to do so convincingly. Good intentions are not enough, if the actions selected do more harm than good. It might even be wise as a matter of principle if professional theologians would stick to declaration of Biblical principles, while lay-persons with the requisite economic training and experience work out the implications and implementations. A preacher may be right to say we ought to assist the poor in a certain place without pretending himself to know how best to achieve that, apart from sacrificial assistance to relieve the immediate necessities. We have had more than enough uninformed rhetoric from church bureaucrats in recent years in support of policies which have proved ruinous.[26] The pursuit of utopia is a betrayal of the poor.

CONCLUSION

Statism is one of the great idols of the modern world. Political redemption or salvation through the gargantuan state, presented under the guise of "social justice," is a deadly myth which Christians ought to oppose.[27] We need to see reality: Facts are facts, and facts dictate that any society with a social conscience should adopt a market approach, with whatever refinements its citizens wish to introduce along the way.

"Liberation" theology has been helpful in reintroducing hope for history into the Christian perspective again, after a century of gloom and doom pessimism. Like the old Reformed post-millennial eschatology, some theologians of the left actually dare to believe that Christ is Lord and can bring the nations under his righteous rule. They spoil that achievement by relying on Marx's theory rather than on

Jesus' word and power, but they do deserve credit for reminding us that in Abraham's seed shall all the nations of earth be blessed with peace, justice, and prosperity. And indeed all the nations will be, thanks be to God!

FIVE

THE FREE ECONOMY
P. T. Bauer's Empirical Analysis
Herbert Schlossberg

*E*conomic liberty has not had a good press in recent decades. Intellectuals from Lenin to Myrdal have associated it with either oppression or inefficiency, and have sought a better society in centralized direction of the economy. Thus the spirit of the age, by and large, has been collectivist, with only a few scholars questioning the consensus. Among these has been P. T. Bauer.

Bauer, a Hungarian by birth, has been associated for many years with the London School of Economics. Like Gunnar Myrdal, Bauer regards himself as a maverick or "dissenter" within economics; the book that established Bauer's reputation in development economics was entitled *Dissent on Development*. But the two dissents are very different in nature. Myrdal, starting with the conviction that planning is essential to economic development, sees centralized government power as our economic savior; Bauer, convinced that economic performance depends on cultural factors and institutional relationships, sees governmental action as one of the chief causes of economic distress. Bauer has been very critical of collectivist ideas in general and Myrdal's ideas in particular, believing that they would lead to "the replacement of human society by a standardized mass, subject to rulers with unlimited power," with society "dehumanized . . . more akin to that of the insects."[1]

To evaluate the two conflicting viewpoints, it's important to see why Bauer arrived at a set of conclusions so completely opposed to political control of the economy. His early studies in the 1940s and 1950s examined the Southeast Asia rubber industry and trade in what was then called British West Africa. From these studies, as well as personal observations made during extended periods in those regions, he found that human differences were crucial; for example, Indians harvested half the rubber that Chinese did when they were working on the same plantations. Such facts taught him not to place so much emphasis on the physical resources available to people, and to pay more attention to the culture and institutions in developing countries. Still, he later concluded that his early work suffered from an inadequate understanding of the detrimental effects of the politicization of economic life, a theme that has been dominant in his more mature writings.[2]

In marked contrast to Myrdal's faith in the efficacy of the economic "church," Bauer argues that economists ought to focus on visible phenomena, and that when they fail to do so they are unable to deal in any depth with the underlying factors that lead to economic progress.[3] Thus he seeks to divert attention away from ideology and toward observation. This empirical approach explains Bauer's efforts to study such seemingly trivial subjects as the official marketing boards that are used to distribute agricultural products in Africa. He concluded that these boards amount to a scheme to tax producers. This takes from farmers their rightful due, while at the same time reducing both production and capital formation and also politicizing ordinary commercial life.[4] This micro-analysis issues from Bauer's empirical orientation and contrasts sharply with Myrdal's focus on macroeconomics.

Since Bauer emphasizes the observable particularities, it is natural for him to reject economic subjectivism and the tendency to politicize personal preferences. He does not accept the belief that economic propositions are necessarily political in nature, and he argues that subjectivism destroys economics as an academic discipline.[5] Instead, he urges that objectively-ascertained economic principles, such as opportunity costs and supply/demand relationships as functions of price, show the way the world works, regardless of the values of the observer. The refusal to distinguish between science and policy leads to incoherence, Bauer argues, and it does incalculable damage to major institutions of Western society. That damage is sometimes the end that is sought.[6]

Bauer argues that much of what passes for wisdom in development economics is "inconsistent with simple empirical observation, with established elementary propositions of economics, and also with widely accepted and well documented ideas of cognate disciplines, notably economic history and social anthropology."[7] The empirical data to which Bauer refers include reports of numerous economic "miracles," successes that the theorists urging centralized planning would find most improbable. Bauer refers in par-

ticular to the economic accomplishments of unenfran-
chised and poor Asians in East Africa. This kind of evidence undermines many common assertions: that it is practically impossible to emerge from poverty without external
aid or state subsidies; that prosperity depends on political
rights or even privileges; that the incomes of better-off
people have been extracted from others, rather than produced by themselves; that trade and services are unproduc-
tive, as opposed to agriculture and manufacturing; and that
economic productivity is a zero-sum game in which gainers
perforce enjoy their benefits at the expense of others.[8]
Bauer contends that those who place economic decisions
with central authorities either ignore or underestimate
both the importance of people's values and capacities, and
the nature of the social institutions that reflect those values.[9]

How does Bauer account for the fact that leaders of an
important sub-discipline have been so blind? He looks primarily at the motivations of the theorists, although he acknowledges that the arguments must stand or fall on their
own without regard for anyone's motives. Some theorists,
he argues, look more at politics than facts; they even regard
the distinction between pursuing knowledge and promot-
ing policy as "fanciful."

Bauer also suggests other reasons for economic failure.
He believes that Marxist influence has become so pervasive
that even those who are not Marxists have picked up some
of its convictions. Much of the development literature is
biased by a general disenchantment with the West, especially on the part of Western intellectuals.[10] On a more
technical note, he also believes that a preoccupation with
the quantifiable blinds many analysts to more important

factors. He mentions, for example, the fact that Asian art, in comparison with that of Europe, emphasizes contemplation and repose, and he suggests that those values are important for understanding economic performance.[11]

Another reason Bauer's conclusions are at variance with consensus development economics is that he looks on the national economies very differently. Many theorists devise schemes for dividing up the national economic pie, but Bauer denies that any such pie exists, and notes that the very image of a pie calls to mind a server cutting it into pieces. If one has more than another, it is only natural to consider that whoever apportioned the pie did so unjustly.[12] In contrast, Bauer concludes that wealth is produced by people in accordance with determinants that are subject to empirical testing. "Economic achievement and progress depend largely on human aptitudes and attitudes, on social and political institutions and arrangements which derive from these, on historical experience, and to a lesser extent on external contacts, market opportunities and on natural resources."[13]

Such an emphasis naturally is less impressed with the accumulation of physical capital than are rival views. He cites recent studies in the United States and England which fail to show correspondence between capital growth and secular income growth, and concludes that the expenditure of money does not achieve much unless it is accompanied by fundamental cultural and institutional changes.[14] Bauer defends income differences as long as they are based on the principle of value given for value received; he equates injustice not with inequality, but with the use of political power in order to gain wealth. Commonly, people are poor because of cultural factors which they choose not to change:

they may insist that women not work outside the home; that animals not be killed; that it is more prestigious not to do physical work; that it is not worth taking risks.[15]

Bauer invites us to make a Copernican sort of reversal in our views of wealth and poverty. If we assume that the wealth of the West is the norm, then we have to explain why most of the world is poor. But since both history and current observation show poverty to be far more common, Bauer suggests that we should seek to understand how it is that in a few odd corners of the world people are not poor.[16] And when we look at some of those corners we find that the oft-cited "vicious cycle of poverty" falls flat, punctured by remarkable progress. The endlessly repeated assertions of a growing gap between rich and poor nations also have no factual validity.[17]

RESPONSIBILITY FOR POVERTY

One of the features of the consensus on development economics is the conviction that the West, and particularly the colonial heritage, has done serious damage to the poor countries. Bauer thinks the consensus view is without foundation, and disagrees in particular with Myrdal on this point. He cites prosperous countries which are or were colonies, and notes that some of the very poorest never were colonies.[18] He calls attention to an incident in which a student group at Cambridge University published a pamphlet on the obligations of the West to the poor countries. This publication supported its thesis with the charge that the British took the rubber from Malaya and the tea from India, while giving almost nothing in return for it. Bauer responds that the truth is precisely the opposite: the British took the rubber *to* Malaya and the tea *to* India. In almost every place Europeans settled, the natives are better off than when they came.[19]

Bauer interprets the spread of the idea of the guilt of the West as a politically inspired ploy to foster the redistribution ideology, since without the assumption of guilt there would be no plausible case for global redistribution. The fact of inequality would be taken as natural.[20] Bauer can argue that inequality is natural because he flatly denies on empirical grounds assertions of the essential equality of all men under nature.[21] The equalitarian error leads people to the idea that aptitudes and motivations are the same, and that sets the stage for serious policy errors.[22]

Bauer's empirical bent leads him to oppose the belief that restricting population is essential to economic development. He finds no correlation between population density and poverty, and concludes that birth control policies are therefore unlikely to increase living standards. He points to large parts of South Asia that are sparsely populated but have low living standards and other places that have high population densities with high living standards.[23]

Bauer emphasizes the relationship of culture and economics. For him, an economy

> consists of people whose material needs it has to satisfy and whose performance largely determines the material achievement of the economy and its rate of advance. This is a platitude. . . . The prime corollary of this platitude is that economic achievement depends primarily on people's abilities and attitudes and also on their social and political institutions.[24]

From this strong emphasis on the personal qualities of human beings, it follows that capital resources are less important than is assumed by many economists; they are a result—a dependent variable—rather than a cause. Bauer thinks it strange that in artistic, athletic, political and intellectual life, the role of personal qualities is recognized, but not in economic life. The reason for this, he believes, is the prevalence of environmental determinism.[25]

Bauer's conclusions follow from his basic premise that economic performance stems from personal qualities and institutional factors. Central planning is not only not necessary, but is more likely to retard development than help it. That is because development requires

> modernization of the mind. It requires revision of the attitudes, modes of conduct and institutions adverse to material progress. The attitudes, mores and institutions of large parts of the underdeveloped world differ radically from those which have promoted the material progress in the west of the last three millennia, especially those which have prevailed in recent centuries.[26]

Thus far this emphasis on culture does not sound very different from Myrdal's position. The differences lies in the consistency with which the principle is applied and the extent to which each man believes it is possible and advisable to change the culture from above. Whereas Myrdal is willing to use coercive means to change the way people live and think, Bauer believes that is a disaster for them. Those attitudes and values in the poor countries may be economically disadvantageous, as well as being an intense frustration to central planners, but they are an integral part of the lives of the people who hold them. To be rid of them by fiat—for example, to prevent people from having large families—could lead to spiritual collapse.[27]

Bauer is suspicious of the model-building quantifiers who neglect the non-quantifiable. He draws our attention to the contemplation and stillness in oriental art, and contrasts it with the restlessness and experimentation in Western art. Bauer believes the prevalence of pantheism profoundly affects economic life, largely because taking an objective view of reality is very difficult to reconcile with a position that regards the mind as having a fundamental unity with nature. The pantheist is likely to display a detachment from worldly affairs, an avoidance of ambition and of concern about external activities, a lack of curiosity, and a general passivity.[28]

Myrdal and Bauer differ about what can be done to assist economic development of people who have those attitudes. Myrdal warns them against adopting uncritically the educational practices and policies of the West.[29] Bauer says forthrightly that such an idea is self-defeating, for "the idea of modernization without Westernization is self-contradictory."[30] The prime case in point for him is the example of Hong Kong, and he devotes a good deal of attention to showing how the culture of Hong Kong—or rather its adoption of Western culture—is what made possible its economic success.[31] Bauer makes this point perhaps most effectively in citing the ideas of a Burundi bishop:

> Bishop Bududira's principal theme is that the local cultures in Africa and elsewhere in the Third World obstruct material progress. The Bishop insists that economic improvement of a person depends on the person

himself, notably on his mental attitudes and especially on his attitude to work. Unquestioning acceptance of nature and of its vagaries is widespread in Africa and elsewhere in the Third World. Man sees himself not as making history but as suffering it. To regard life as inexorably ordained by fate prevents a person from developing his or her potential. . . . The Bishop concludes that the message of Christ frees people from the shackles of tribal thinking, and leads to a greater sense of personal responsibility. The required changes can best be achieved by Christian groups working with local communities.[32]

Bauer's understanding of the role of the elite comes from seeing what they actually do. He shows that they are the chief beneficiaries of their own actions. The power implied by the controls and planning accrues to *them*. They have private agendas that are commonly masked by the language of public service and social benefit; they frequently acquire not only power but also great wealth.[33] James Buchanan received the Nobel prize in economics in 1986, long after Bauer expressed these views, for studies demonstrating that public officials ordinarily devise policies that benefit themselves.

Bauer objects to the fact that it is taken for granted, without demonstration, that central planning is necessary and markets exercise insufficient control over economic life. When he undertook a lecture tour of a dozen universities and research institutes in India in 1970, the students and faculty members all assumed that there could be no rise in living standards without central planning; the only question was whether it was to be the Soviet or the Chinese model.[34] Bauer, again citing evidence, shows that central planning has played no role in the development of the West and of Japan or the other prosperous nations of Asia.[35]

It would be bad enough if central planning, costly as it is, made no contribution to development. But Bauer shows that it actually hinders economic advance. Controls require placing of inhibitions on people in countries where the inhibitions from cultural phenomena are already great.[36] Bauer's early primary research was in commodity stabilization plans and marketing boards in Africa, both examples of central planning; he returns again and again to the damage done to the people by these institutions.[37] In describing all this, he confirms the observations of Myrdal that the government is ordinarily captured by commercial and political interests which profit from the controls that impoverish the masses. Unlike Myrdal, however, he draws the logical conclusions and labels the regimes he is describing as *kleptocracies* (borrowing the term from S. L. Andreski).[38]

Rather than regarding the bad effects of foreign aid as a paradox, Bauer says that these unforeseen problems are only to be expected. He even observes that, typically, aid results in the destruction of capital; that is, the output is less than the input of the aid that was received. Normally, this occurs because of actions taken by the recipient governments, and the aid is what makes those actions possible.[39] Perhaps the most serious result of foreign aid is the development of attitudes inimical to development. It encourages people to look to outside help rather than recognizing that their economic performance is dependent on themselves. They thus learn to expect "success without achievement, to believe that material reward depends on windfalls, and to want the results of economic success without the antecedent process."[40]

Moreover, the lack of ambition often seen in poor groups is reinforced by handouts, thus making it more likely that the people will fall into the state of pauperization. That is what happened in the U.S. trusteeship of Micronesia. As the Washington *Post* reported this disaster:

> US trusteeship in Micronesia has created a society dependent on government jobs and benefits, an island welfare state whose people are so inundated with handouts that they are abandoning even those elemental enterprises—fishing and farming—that they had developed before the Americans came.
>
> "We've smothered them," said a veteran US administrator with the trust territory government, "and it will take them a long time to come out from under the blanket. . . ."
>
> "Any kind of work here is very hard work," said . . . an economist with the trust government, "and now you can live here without working. . . ."
>
> The US administration is universally blamed for the islanders' dependency, even by current administrators. The only argument is over whether the United States deliberately conspired to promote it or merely bungled in its humanitarian zeal. . . .
>
> The Kennedy administration poured in funds for education, health, and welfare. Since then, annual appropriations for Micronesia have risen from about $5 million to about $100 million, and $30 million more is given yearly to the inhabitants on categorical programs such as food, special education and direct welfare.[41]

Bauer's work consistently attacks the easy justification of coercion typical among modern theorists. He is very critical of Third-World political forces that try to direct every aspect of their peoples' lives, and also of the Western governments that help them do so. His point here is not that individual rights are more important than the economic development that will accrue to poor countries amid coercion. Rather, he believes that coercion is a major reason for development's *failure* to take place. No central planner, no matter how fortified with computers, can possibly know the needs, preferences, prospects and opportunities of the citizens better than they themselves can.[42] Thus Bauer draws on the body of economic theory which sees markets as, among other things, information-imparting devices that not only satisfy wants but allow people to plan rationally for the needs of others as well as their own.

Bauer also exposes regimes that have repressed the people of poor countries, including some of those that have been most strongly praised by Western progressive thinkers. The brutality of the Nyerere regime in Tanzania is a subject of special attention, largely because it is so strongly supported by institutions like the World Bank and the foreign aid budgets of the Scandinavian countries. He thinks it is a mistake for the West to give foreign aid without strings, because restrictions and accountability may be all that protect the populations from their governments.[43] Like Myrdal, Bauer emphasizes the way foreign aid leads to the politicization of economic life, with benefits cascading upon the rich, further impoverishment of the poor, and endemic corruption. The two economists are largely in agreement on these intermediate questions and yet disagree on the conclusions that should be inferred from their common answers.

A major reason for the difference is that Bauer insists that the economic data have to be taken seriously, refusing to burden them with ideological baggage. As we would expect, his work is much less value-laden than Myrdal's, but he does provide clues that tell us something of his values. He is critical, for example, of the single-minded pursuit of increased income. Per capita income is reduced by both births and medicines, but people like to have children and would prefer to have them remain alive. Bauer is not unhappy that children are valued, and he does not believe it justifiable for planners to violate religious and ethical convictions in order to raise income.[44] But Bauer stops short of specifying what the values that inform policy ought to be. That leaves the reader uncertain as to his foundational assumptions. In a world of economists who often substitute ideology for evidence, from what source does Bauer's empirical orientation derive? We do not know. Nor can we easily determine the philosophical filters through which the raw data are filtered.

IMPERATIVES FOR ECONOMIC DEVELOPMENT

Herbert Schlossberg

*B*auer's work shows the importance of critically assessing ideas that deal with economic development. Christians will be able to act more constructively in this area only as we think in a way that is true to our own traditions and cease accepting uncritically ideas on development advanced by experts who disagree with the fundamentals of Christian faith. Expertise is almost always mixed with value judgments based on worldviews. The experts give us information and recommendations produced not only by scientific investigation, but also by the beliefs of the investigators and by those who interpret their findings. Even if we use this information well, we may come to the wrong conclusions, because the "facts" on which we are relying may be dependent upon false ideologies.

THE IMPORTANCE OF INTELLECTUAL FOUNDATIONS

When Gunnar Myrdal says he is an Enlightenment philosopher he is telling the truth, and he is being more honest than most people who have his convictions. Whether or not the source of beliefs is identified so clearly, it's essential for Christians using expert testimony to examine critically the assumptions that provide the basis for such testimony. But what difference does it make that Myrdal is an Enlightenment philosopher? Or that another expert is a pantheist, another a behaviorist, another a Marxist, another a Malthusian? It makes all the difference in the world.

For an illustration of why that is so, we might consider the recent analysis of a professor of biology at a Christian college who was considering the problem of economic need in poor countries. He accepted uncritically sources that were bound to lead him astray, particularly the grim prognostications of the early nineteenth-century prophet Thomas Malthus that have been resurrected in our day and given a scientific covering. Malthus believed that the population of the earth was increasing geometrically, but the food supplies were increasing only arithmetically. Therefore, it would be only a matter of time until the mouths to be fed exceeded the supply of available food, and the result would be mass starvation.

In recent years, national and international organizations have busied themselves with this idea, using Malthus's assumptions but updating them with high-speed computation and modern concerns. Adding the problem of pollution to resource deficiencies and overpopulation, the situation seems hopeless indeed. Documents such as the Club of Rome reports, the Brandt Commission report, and Global

2000 contain all the pessimism that frightened Malthus's readers almost two centuries ago. And this Christian biologist accepted it all.[1]

How can we protect ourselves against such errors? Well, for one thing we can read the literature more carefully. Anybody with even the most basic knowledge of economics would question seriously whether the Malthusian horror of widespread food shortages could be taking place in a world in which agricultural and other commodity prices have been plunging for several years. Furthermore, neo-Malthusianism is a heavily criticized ideology, and it is not difficult to find counterarguments showing the shakiness of the science which leads people to such pessimistic conclusions. Concerned about the needless alarm the neo-Malthusians were raising, and their support for destructive policy recommendations, Julian Simon and Herman Kahn collected the writings of specialists in the fields of physics, economics, nutrition, geography, mathematics, biology, demographics, forestry, geophysics, agriculture, political science and oceanography. Taken together, this work showed the neo-Malthusian science to be false.[2] That is only a sample of the kind of counter-information available to us.

We are not limited to the task of comparing the conflicting arguments of scientists, many of which we will not even be able to understand. If we analyze the assumptions implicit (sometimes explicit) in the neo-Malthusian writings, we can observe that they are utterly naturalistic. They show no understanding that the earth was created by a just and loving God, that its resources are not going to "run out" before their Creator intends, that the exercise of stewardship is not in conflict with the responsibilities that God has placed upon us. The failure to get straight the bad theology of those sources—including sources that don't claim to have a theology—places Christians who rely on them in an impossible situation. They try to follow the Biblical commandments using ideas that are completely pagan in origin.

The result of such an attempt is frustration and failure. Perhaps the most common characteristic of the false perspectives that deal with the issue of economic development is their utopianism. We observe that if resources were spread around the world more evenly nobody would be in want. It seems to follow that what is wrong is the social organization that causes such maldistribution. From this it seems natural to say that the problem can be solved if we change the social organization. The final inference is a full-blown plan for the restructuring of a world in which those sad disturbances are restructured out of existence.

Many modern prescriptions for social reform borrow much from that sort of utopian thinking. They are often based upon an anthropology that lacks the richness and realism of the Biblical doctrine of man. Rather than recognizing that God created us in His image, and that that image is marred by our sin, these theories often assume that we're automatons, obediently responding to whatever manipulation of the environment our betters plan for us. The fact that we are not so constituted accounts for the intense frustration evident in Gunnar Myrdal's writings: The planners plan, but we decline to react as they expect. The collapse of all the marvels of central planning in the Communist world, and the present humiliating effort to rely on market mechanisms in their place, is another manifestation of the same phenomenon.

DEVELOPMENT STRATEGIES CONSISTENT WITH A BIBLICAL WORLDVIEW

The way to economic health begins with the recognition that human beings are not simply creatures of nature, fully subservient to our environments. We are created in the image of God, and are therefore unique in all the creation. We respond to situations in terms of values, not just instincts; and these values are, among other characteristics, both internal and transcendent.

The purveyors of utopian fantasies that are doing so much damage to human societies have a different view of humanity. They attribute the ills that people suffer to various aspects of the environment: climate, lack of capital, failure of governments to take this or that action, betrayal by foreign powers, and so on. The preferred explanation is always something extraneous to the sufferers and, wherever possible, extraneous to the countrymen of the sufferers. Their assumption is clear: humanity is fully a part of nature, and can be fully explained by that fact. People are as subject to external forces as any other part of nature. There is no room in this conception for moral action, and that is why ethical thinking plays so little role in mainstream economic development theory. That is also why *culture*—a peculiarly human manifestation—is so seldom thought to play any significant role in development.

In Biblical perspective, however, economics is primarily a moral science. It is a science because it has data to be studied, hypotheses to be tested, predictive value, and a systematic body of knowledge. But the fact that it is loaded with normative information makes economics fundamentally different from, say, mathematics. We see repeatedly in the Bible that the economic material has moral content. It is not the case, as so many have thought, that the Biblical message on economics is that we work hard and save our money and thereby become prosperous. Rather, the message is that we reap the consequences of what we sow, and that reaping has an economic component to it:

> Shall I acquit a man with dishonest scales, with a bag of false weights? Her rich men are violent; her people are liars and their tongues speak deceitfullly. Therefore, I have begun to destroy you, to ruin you because of your sins. You will eat but not be satisfied; your stomach will still be empty. You will store up but save nothing, because what you save I will give to the sword. You shall plant, but not harvest; you shall press olives, but not use the oil on yourselves, you shall crush grapes, but not drink the wine. (Mic. 6:11-15)

The people described here worked hard, saved their money, and still ended up poor. They fell into the materialist fallacy of thinking that wealth came from purely economic activities; thus they were rich with their planting and watering and saving, and despised the God who gave them the economic resources in the first place. Over a sufficient period of time, societies that live in ways other than God intended for humanity see the work of their hands destroyed. The moral condition overrides the others.

But moral arguments can be misused. Some of those who expound most insistently on the responsibilities Christians have to help the poor offer policy recommendations that almost seem calculated to damage the poor. They seem to conclude that there is an easy step from quoting a gospel verse about the poor to arriving at a public policy.

Even if it is true that such passages are intended to inform public policies, there are intermediate steps that must be taken before we arrive at the knowledge of those policies. Prudential matters have to be related to moral principles, but they are not identical with them. Someone reads that we are obliged to give to the poor and concludes from this that the minimum wage must be raised. The uplifted feeling that comes from taking so virtuous a position does not compensate for all the poor people thrown out of work by the policy. Numerous other policies that seem self-evidently to be inferred from Biblical principles are equally destructive.

We would do better at this if our own motives were on firmer ground. People plagued by guilt feelings are not good candidates to be making recommendations for economic development.[3] When they do, they tend to parrot World Bank presidents and oppressors of Third-World populations with their calls for ever-greater income transfers as the road to development. Christ has paid the penalty for our sins, and we do not come to the issues covered with guilt. We can look at the situation with clear eyes, because we are not trying to save ourselves through self-abasement. Humility is sufficient; breast-beating is superfluous and suggests a sub-Christian doctrine of salvation.

DISCERNING OPPRESSION WHEN IT OCCURS

Thus placed on solid ground, we can look more clearly at one characteristic of many poor countries that emerges from analysts as different as Myrdal and Bauer: rampant injustice in governance. This is a formidable barrier to economic health, since few people are willing to build a business or even a house if an arbitrary ruling is likely to take it away. Although arbitrary administrative and legal decisions can take place virtually anywhere, they are endemic in many poor countries. Corruption is found at every level of official life in those places. Nobody gets approval for anything without paying bribes.

This brings special hardship wherever the reigning theory and practice is statist. Where liberty is honored and protected, people don't need rubber stamps on permits for many of the ordinary affairs of life. But where the voice of virtue assumes that such stamps serve to protect the people or create justice, that sets the stage for arbitrary rulings and rampant corruption. A common Biblical word, "oppression," describes such a situation. Quite often the Biblical passages that denounce oppression are mistakenly thought to be talking about overcoming poverty—usually through reapportioning income—which is a very different thing.[4] But such a reading cuts the heart out of those very stern and demanding parts of the Bible, and makes it seem like a social democratic manifesto.

When the prophets denounced oppression, they were not speaking of what percentage of the national income was earned by those in the lowest quintile of the population, in the manner of modern humanitarians and their academic, ecclesiastic, and government spokesmen. They were talking about stealing the land belonging to others, denying them justice in the courts, taking the bread from widows and orphans, and so on. Governments all over the world are doing such things today. This is seldom recognized by those who see economic problems purely in terms of "poverty." Yet, the realities of the present are scarcely different from those of three millennia ago:

If you see the poor oppressed in a district, and justice
and rights denied, do not be surprised at such things; for
one official is eyed by a higher one, and over them both
are others higher still. The increase from the land is
taken by all; the king himself profits from the fields.
(Ecc. 5:8ff.)

It might be supposed that nothing should be easier
than discerning oppression, but contemporary history
shows otherwise. One of the recent heroes of Westerners
who claim to support the economic rights of people in
poor countries is Julius Nyerere, who was until a short
time ago President of Tanzania (and is still head of the
ruling party there). His special champion was Robert Mc-
Namara, former president of the World Bank, and McNa-
mara pressed the Bank's resources on Tanzania with abandon. The Scandinavian governments were also strong fi-
nancial and political supporters of his policies. Unhappily,
Christians have joined the chorus. When the Oxford Conference on Christian Faith and Economics, meeting early in
1987, cast about for a keynote speaker they settled on
Nyerere for the honor (although, as it turned out, he could
not attend).

What had Nyerere done to attract so much favorable
attention? When he came to power he essentially national-
ized the Tanzanian economy. In 1967 he introduced a central planning system based on the Chinese model. He established hundreds of communal villages, and when the
peasants refused to go to them he had the army truck the
recalcitrants in forcibly. Some peasants who resisted had
their houses burned or bulldozed. Nyerere called for one-

man, one-vote politics in southern Africa, but he allowed no political party in Tanzania apart from his own. His jails were full of political prisoners, and Amnesty International reported torture by Tanzanian officials. Not content with his policies at home, Nyerere overthrew the governments of three other African nations.

With all the foreign money pumped into Tanzania—more, per capita, than any African nation and probably second in that regard only to India—the economy has gone steadily downhill. Agricultural prices are set so low by the government that the peasants cannot make a living by producing food, so they refrain from production.[5] So desperate has the situation become that Michael Lofchie, director of the African Studies Center at UCLA, reports it in almost apocalyptic terms:

> Even its most ardent defenders acknowledge an economic failure of such calamitous proportions that meaningful recovery may well be impossible. Critics foresee an even bleaker future: continued economic deterioration characterized by increasingly frequent episodes of famine, further disintegration of the infrastructure, the virtual disappearance of basic social services (once the country's principal source of self-esteem) and an atmosphere of corruption, cynicism and powerlessness on the part of the country's political elite.[6]

How then could so many Western leaders puff the Nyerere regime as an example to the world? Why was Nyerere feted and invited to lecture all over the West? How could the bankers and politicians have pressed on Tanzania such huge sums of cash—cash that was to be swallowed up in waste, corruption and oppression? Why would Christian academic and business leaders, concerned about economic justice in relation to Christian faith, invite such a man to address them?

Several reasons come to mind. To a certain extent the practice of economics has been so highly infected by ideology that the words a leader uses seem to have more import than the actions he takes. Nyerere, having learned Fabian socialism at the University of Edinburgh, knew the language calculated to elicit foreign support. He repeatedly described foreign aid not as charity but as a matter of justice, implying that those who gave it *owed* it. Guilty consciences swoon at this kind of talk.

Ignorance also plays a part. One of the leaders of the Oxford Conference responded to a question by saying that he and his colleagues invited Nyerere to give the keynote address because they knew he was Catholic. Thus, a profession of Christian faith was taken to be sufficient for serving as a role model and teacher on the question of development economics. The fact that Nyerere presided over a tyranny remained undiscovered. Christians involved in the public policy debate cannot help the world's poor with that kind of inattention to what is actually happening in poor countries.

We need to look more closely at action and not rely on rhetoric. The lawlessness that allows soldiers to move poor people from their land to camps that the government thinks are more suitable for them is not only unjust in itself, but makes it improbable that people will build economic structures that the society needs. The subjection of those structures to government whim, along with the likelihood that the fruits of labor will be taken away at the next turn of the political wheel, frustrates enterprise. What rational person would expend the capital and labor to clear farmland if he suspected that before the next harvest the state would present the property to someone else? Who would build a house while doubting that the courts would secure the title? Who would start a business in a country in which contracts are awarded on the basis of political pull? Why would anyone plant a cash crop where price controls and government marketing boards insure that the cost to the farmer of raising the crop exceeds the income it returns? The answer to those questions appears in an extreme form in Tanzania, but almost every poor country exhibits an advanced case of the same characteristics.

It should be no surprise that World Bank presidents and politicians overlook these essentially moral issues. For much of the Western worldview has departed from its Christian roots and has adopted a materialist ideology. Believers in that worldview assume that material affairs are at the base of economic life, and have difficulty understanding that moral issues are more fundamental. But no theory of economic development that claims to be informed by Christian faith can afford to adopt that thinking.

The kind of evidence we have been considering suggests ways we can help people in poor countries, along with immediate relief work to deal with life-threatening situations. To begin with, even if we only avoid doing destructive things (following the physician's pledge to "do no harm"), we shall improve matters considerably. We should refrain from assisting the government foreign aid establishment that sends funds which only strengthen the hand of oppressors against their people.[7] The political and economic elite of poor countries are doing well enough at that without us. The moral high ground that has been seized by those who favor such policies has done incalculable harm by turning marginal situations into desperate ones. These negative actions are not enough to bring justice to these unfortunate lands, but we are not going to be able to help much before we stop acting in complicity with tyranny.

Perhaps the single most important task for Christians is to take seriously the Biblical worldview with respect to economic life. In the economic realm this means, almost more than anything, rejecting the current gloomy thinking that sees increasing shortages as the inevitable result of large numbers of people clashing with diminishing resources and with pollution. That view requires, in some fearful attempt to delay our certain doom, that we redistribute what resources we have.

In recent years, the already prevalent pessimism of the neo-Malthusians has been supplemented by theorists such as Jeremy Rifkin who are making an economic principle out of the second law of thermodynamics. This says that the energy sources of the earth are running down—that is, moving from a usable state to an unusable state—through a process called *entropy*, and when that process runs its course life will end. But to order our lives on the basis of an abstract physical principle is to repeat the materialist fallacy. As economic columnist Warren Brookes points out, it is harder to imagine a universe less governed by entropy than one in which manna comes from heaven, water gushes from a struck rock, and the multitudes are fed by a few loaves of bread and a couple of fish. And what about resurrection—does it make sense for one who believes in *that* to pay any attention to Malthusian or entropic piffle?[8]

CHRISTIAN DISCIPLESHIP AND ECONOMIC DEVELOPMENT

If such factors as work, stewardship, an orientation to the future, the honoring of contracts, respect for the property of others, investment, saving and the control of consumption, the integrity of the family, mutual respect in exchanges, and similar factors are essential ingredients in a healthy economic system, then it is clear that *culture* is central to the whole process. And central to culture is the religious vision that informs the culture. That is perhaps the easiest way to grasp how delusive is the materialism that governs so much thinking on economics.

Yet, church documents dealing with economic issues routinely say little or nothing about such issues. To cite a recent example, a number of church leaders convened in Sao Paulo, Brazil, in March 1987 for a meeting called "Confessing Movements and Economic Justice," under the sponsorship of the World Council of Churches and the Lutheran World Federation. The conference report tells of the terrible oppression that afflicts people in such benighted places as Brazil, the Netherlands, New York, and South Africa, but says nothing whatever of the cultural factors that bear on poverty. Thus we have the odd phenomenon of religious organizations which act as if religion has no effect on economic life. (This document is also highly selective in its indignation. There is only one passing reference to Eastern Europe that the alert reader might use to guess something about the wholesale repression under Communist regimes. And the African National Congress is puffed as part of the resistance movement to apartheid, with no mention of its murderous terror campaign against blacks who do not agree with it.)

If church bodies like this one had their way, there would be a massive transfer of resources from rich countries to poor ones, because they are ignorant of the near certainty that there would be no long-term benefit to the recipients. Why is it that Nation A is prosperous and Nation B is poverty-stricken? According to the materialist dogma, it must be that the first is well supplied with natural resources, a fertile land, and a productive infrastructure, such as a good educational system, modern factories, roads, and public works. If Nation B lacks all these things naturally, it is going to be poor. To set matters right, it is only necessary to transfer resources to it.

Yet the experience of such countries as Japan, which have few resources but are wealthy, and Brazil, which is loaded with resources but is poor, shows that cannot be the case. This analysis by itself should be enough to demonstrate the falsity of the materialist assumption. At the end of World War II, Germany and Japan were prostrate. But in less than a generation they had become economic powerhouses. It seems likely that if they could transport virtually their entire economic structure to a Brazil in some massive redistribution, in another generation Japan would again be rich and Brazil poor. The persistent failure of so many Christian churches and organizations to consider the cultural causes of poverty is especially galling because there is hardly a feature in the preceding paragraph describing a healthy culture that is not specified in the Bible as a requirement for those who are to be faithful to God.

The testimony of a number of Christians in West Germany who have recently emigrated from the Soviet Union provides additional illustrations of the centrality of culture for economic performance. Mostly factory workers from Central Asia, these people suffered many forms of prejudice in their towns and workplaces, but they won sincere admiration from foremen and managers at the factories because they *worked*. In a society in which drunkenness, sloth, and theft from the workplace seriously weaken economic performance, these Christians had a Biblical attitude toward sobriety, labor and honesty. They were routinely selected for tasks that had to be done without supervision.[9] Just now, some seventy years after their revolution, the Soviet regime is blaming the abysmal performance of their economy partially on the poor characteristics of their work force. That they should have made the error for so long is a reflection of the fact that they rejected the Christian worldview, with its anthropology, and sought explanations elsewhere.

Marxist ideology is not the only source of error and hardship. A society that values leisure more than work, that considers it prestigious to be indolent, will tend to have the most ambitious people seeking to do nothing. Special talents, rather than serving the society and the people, will, if the person is successful in attaining his ambitions, accomplish nothing at all. Whether a whole culture tends toward sloth or industry makes a great difference in how it performs. Those who think economic standing comes only from material factors, or who seek answers only in external circumstances, will never understand these realities. There is no point in blaming outside agencies if the ideology that drives the people is such that renders them ineffective, indolent, selfish, profligate, venal, lawless, short-sighted, or having other qualities that prevent them from mutual service in a healthy economy.

Perhaps the most dramatic evidence in American society of the connection between cultural factors and economic well-being lies in the family life of the urban black ghettos. The demographic group most at risk is that composed of single and divorced men. These men have almost twice the mortality rate of married men and three times that of single women. Single men are far more likely to fall into poverty, depression, crime, alcoholism, drug abuse and AIDS. And the longer a man goes without marrying, the likelier he is to kill himself.

But the young men of the ghetto culture, full of energies that could not be tamed and ignorance that could not be erased by a failing school system, are not considered bargains in the economy of marriage to the single women who bear their children and are supported by the welfare system. Nor are the men, ignorant of the long-term costs of their situation, anxious to lose what they think is their freedom. Thus the governmental support structure undergirds a destructive cultural pattern that is all the more tenacious because it is subsidized. Young men lack the stabilizing influence of close ties to wives and children, and young mothers face the extraordinarily difficult task of raising their children alone. It's no wonder that the pathologies are being reproduced along with the succeeding generations.[10]

What about societies that are not Christian but which do well economically? We do not lack for examples of such nations, whose cultures are consonant with Biblical teaching and who are therefore prosperous. To some extent this is due to the common grace by which God provides for and enlightens all people, the factor which Paul says leaves all "without excuse" (Rom. 1:20). But it is also the case that the gospel is a blessing even to those who do not accept it. After U.S. gunboat diplomacy opened Japanese society to the West in the nineteenth century, Japan consciously copied Western cultures—their dress, customs and so on. The culture of Victorian Britain—an evangelical Protestant culture—in particular was the model of choice. That is why it is not absurd to regard modern Japan as in some sense embodying a Protestant worldview, although the country has not been particularly receptive to Christian mission work.

The gospel benefits even those who do not accept it, but our commission is to make disciples of all nations (Matt. 28:19). The notion that economic concerns are competitive with mission work, that our concern for the poor must be at the expense of our preaching and vice versa, is a goofy idea that has done great damage to both economic development and mission work. It is based on a misreading of the Biblical material and also a misapprehension of economic life. It is dependent on the idea of a radical dualism between the spiritual and material, a failure to recognize the Biblical teaching that Christian discipleship has a profound effect on all of life. To the extent that the culture of a people is responsible for its poverty, that nation needs the transformation of the gospel. To the extent that oppression is the cause of poverty, the same cure is needed, along with a political effort to bring about justice. G. K. Chesterton once remarked that the quietism of the pantheist has never overthrown a tyrant.

The most effective means of spreading economic development, therefore, is a full-orbed mission program. It would preach and teach the gospel, but that would have a far broader meaning than is commonly thought to be the case. Along with the transforming power of regeneration, such a gospel would teach the doctrine of serving the Creator rather than the creation. It would stress Biblical principles of family, work, capital and stewardship, worship and church life, self-control and generosity, consumption and debt. It would view nature as God's handiwork without worshiping it, and teach love for one's neighbor along with the expectation that the neighbor would work for his family and others.

Any nation that believed and practiced a gospel such as this would not be the recipient of Western charity for long. Instead it would leave the increasingly neo-pagan West in the dust, and it would be ministering health to other countries. Perhaps it would be sending missionaries to the United States.

THE BEGINNING
OF HOPE

Marvin Olasky

*W*hy must we examine worldviews in connection with questions of international relief and development? Why not just deliver the food and leave? Recently the Milwaukee *Journal*, with uncommon journalistic enterprise, sent two reporters to Asia and Latin America to investigate problems of poverty. Working independently, each reporter came up with evidence pointing to five similar conclusions. Together, those conclusions show the importance of worldview.

First, the journalists found rampant fatalism among the poor. Reporter Meg Kissinger wrote that women in Recife, Brazil, "spoke matter-of-factly about child deaths—the way we would talk about how a bad summer rain has hurt our geraniums. It's a shame, but what are you going to do?" Reporter Richard Kenyon wrote from Bangladesh that when a child is ill, "the child just dies, and the mother has only to say it was Allah's will."[1]

Second, both reporters found a belief that evil spirits

rule the world. Kenyon told of how Shanti Ram Devi, a woman in Nepal,

> was cleaning the stains of diarrhea from the bottom and legs of her 3-year-old daughter in a pool near her home outside the village of Bhalam. . . . "What caused the diarrhea?" I asked. "Ghosts," she said with a look that said my question was foolish. I pointed to the stagnant film and feces floating in the pool of water and asked if that might have anything to do with her daughter's illness. Shanti Ram Devi looked at me blankly.[2]

Third, both reporters found lack of respect for family. Kissinger, in Brazilian slums, wrote that "This is a world where a man is encouraged to father as many children as he can but is branded a homosexual if he takes any part in caring for them."[3] She wanted to interview one father, but he "jumped out of the window when I arrived. He . . . does not help support the children. . . . He went off with his friends to play cards and drink."[4] Kenyon, in Bangladesh, wrote of women abandoned by their husbands through the Moslem practice of divorce, which requires only that a husband say the word for "divorce" three times in order to abandon his wife.[5]

Fourth, both reporters saw many kinds of valuable work shunned, even when the refusal to work can lead to death or disease. Kenyon described a filthy clinic in Nepal, with black, stagnant water in a sink and dirty rags littering a floor. Lower castes within the Hindu caste system were supposed to do the job, but they were not encouraged to work hard or told about the importance of cleanliness, particularly in medical clinics. "Why not educate them or get someone else to do the cleaning?" Kenyon asked an official; the official "shrugged his shoulders, unconcerned and bored with the discussion."[6]

Fifth, both reporters then denied the evidence of their own senses and laid considerable blame for conditions on Americans. Kenyon attacked American-owned garment factories in Bangladesh that pay low wages by American standards, even though workers in those factories earn more than they could otherwise. He attacked "American anti-abortionists" who have tried to keep U.S. family planning grants from subsidizing abortion in Bangladesh.[7] Kissinger, in Brazil, similarly saw abortion as salvation, and then attacked American companies that do business in Brazil.[8]

The reporters concluded their seven-part series with an article headlined "What Can Stop the Dying?"[9] They emphasized population control and transfer of resources from Western countries to others, partly as restitution for supposed past damages. "Colonialists from Europe," Kenyon and Kissinger wrote, "upset cultures and undermined established economies, setting the stage for poverty"[10] —as if poverty did not previously exist in Africa, Asia and Latin America. They recommended increased foreign aid to, and decreased corporate investment in, poorer countries. They criticized "religious groups" that "came to the Third World in the name of helping but with hidden agendas of religious conversion."[11]

"Be ever hearing, but never understanding; be ever seeing, but never perceiving" (Isa. 6:9).[12] The reporters could see the results of not believing in a sovereign and holy God—including a sense of fatalism, worship of evil spirits, and so on. The reporters could see the results of not abiding by Biblical principles in relation to family and work. But they could not make sense of what they saw, because they lacked a Christian perspective. Unable to make sense and casting around for villains, they fell back on the old anti-Western myths that P. T. Bauer has debunked.

THE CHALLENGE TO CHRISTIANS

If Christians see problems of international poverty through twentieth-century materialist glasses, we will make similar errors. We will miss the social and economic significance of a belief that evil spirits rule the world and need to be placated. We will miss the importance of seeing that all human beings operate within God's covenant and deserve respect, since all of us, though scarred by sin, are created in God's image.

The Villars consultation was designed to help us not just to look but to see, and then to understand. Pierre Berthoud set us off in the right direction with an examination of *covenant*. He observes that hunger and deprivation are most terrible because they scar the image of God that is man. The Christian goal is redemption, which requires both spiritual and physical transformation. As covenant-breakers we are responsible for our own behavior, and those who dig a pit will inevitably fall into it. As individuals saved by God's mercy, we need to be merciful enough to throw one end of the rope into that pit, hold on to the other, and pray that God will give the captive strength to climb up.

The idea of *covenant*, Berthoud notes, is central to the Biblical definition of justice. Biblical justice is not a subset of mathematics, with certain precise income distributions viewed as praiseworthy. Instead, Biblical justice is based on telling the truth and following God's Word, regardless of socioeconomic consequences. Two verses in Exodus 23 state this understanding most succinctly: "Do not show favoritism to a poor man in his lawsuit," and "Do not deny justice to your poor people in their lawsuits" (23:3, 6). Those verses are included among others dealing with the importance of truth-telling: "Do not spread false reports. Do not help a wicked man by being a malicious witness. . . . Do not pervert justice by siding with the crowd. . . . Have nothing to do with a false charge. . . . Do not accept a bribe, for a bribe blinds those who see and twists the words of the righteous" (23:1, 2, 7, 8).

Prophets such as Amos attacked bribe-taking and lying, including the use of dishonest weights and measures: "You oppress the righteous and take bribes," he roared against Israel's judges, "and you deprive the poor of justice in the courts" (Amos 5:12). Amos' goal, Berthoud points out, was not to redistribute income, but to make sure those who worked received the wages they had been promised and the goods they had paid for, without those in power practicing legal theft through governmental control.

If Biblical justice means *fairness*, not some kind of imposed mathematical "equality," what then is the Biblical relation of justice, freedom, and international relief and development activities? Herbert Schlossberg's examination of Gunnar Myrdal suggests that the goal of spreading around resources evenly always seems to require coercive means. "Engineered Reconstruction" fails in practice because it underestimates man's need for freedom and our unwillingness to be reprogrammed in accordance with planning objectives. Freedom is essential to our lives, not an add-on to be allowed only after other needs are met.

Schlossberg notes that the anthropology of modern social reform lacks the richness and realism of the Biblical doctrine of man. Instead of recognizing that God created us in His image, social planning theories tend to see man as determined, responding to environmental manipulation. Myrdal and other planners failed to realize that man, created after God's image, needs the freedom to be creative. Creativity is encouraged only when liberties of enterprise and conscience are present. The planners have, of course, also failed to recognize that they themselves suffer from original sin and tend to redouble their efforts as they lose sight of their goals.

Perhaps Myrdal has been so popular because his own output has been high-minded rhetoric rather than bloody action; Clark Pinnock, through his hard look at utopian failures in practice, reminds us of the reality of coercion. Pinnock points out that Marxist-Leninists have brought neither freedom nor justice to societies they have conquered, and have managed to kill the high hopes that usually accompanied their seizure of power. In communism there is no god but our twentieth-century Caesar, the Communist Party—so there can be no covenant, no sense of absolute right and wrong, no freedom to act outside Party constraints. Other forms of Marxism, in their search to not only interpret the world but change it, inevitably are driven to coercion and dictatorship.

Pinnock also notes that Marxist theory (and its soft side, liberation theology) is as flawed as Marxist practice. An emphasis on class struggle cannot possibly come to grips with the devastating reality of sin and evil in all their forms, including pain, suffering, disease, decay, death, and fundamentally, separation from God. Some, of course, argue that although liberation *theology* might be wrong, liberation *economics* is correct in that the Marxist critique in general is accurate and can be a useful tool for Christians. Yet, even if it were possible to divorce economics from theology, the bankruptcy of Marxist economics has become as evident as the bankruptcy of the Marxist worldview generally. Pinnock's evidence shows the importance of another theme that ran throughout the Villars consultation: the necessity to look closely at what actually goes on, and not just to comfort ourselves with faith in our own abstract reason. Actual results show the nature of the world that God has created and man has governed, often for worse, sometimes for better.

Christians must look at the record, Herbert Schlossberg insists. His study of P. T. Bauer's work is particularly helpful in showing how Bauer concentrates on what *has* happened, not on what we wish had happened. Over and over again centralized control of political and economic power has increased suffering rather than alleviated it. Over and over again foreign aid has seldom reached those for whom it was intended, and has usually resulted in an increase of central control, thus hindering economic development, underwriting destructive national policies, and reducing individual freedom.

Schlossberg shows that Bauer's evidence connects non-Christian worldviews with poverty: Cultural values, including resignation in the face of poverty, lack of personal responsibility, and preference for leisure or contemplation over work, are critical. Some economies that fail have at their root theologies that stress performance of duties rather than achievement of results; other failures come when charity has no stigma and enterprise brings no praise. Belief that attempts to transform nature bring retribution from occult forces, or that perpetual reincarnation makes this life less important, kills spiritually *and* physically.

Bauer's analysis is magnificent as far as it goes—but, as Schlossberg suggests, it should go further. Bauer stands for part of the Biblical idea of freedom, the ability to be creative after God's image and not merely a pawn of governments and other powers. He understands the twentieth-century misuse of the word "justice." But where, in Bauer's analysis, is hope?

When Bauer visited the University of Texas late in 1987, he was as reticent as ever about his personal beliefs. He strongly attacked foreign aid, arguing that the greatest hope for the dictator-ridden states of Africa is an overthrow of their leadership, and that "if we had not been giving massive foreign aid, they [the dictators] would have been brought down years ago." Bauer's values emerged slightly when he reacted to one professor's praise of "successful" population control programs: "If you think it is a success forcing women to have abortions, I must disagree with you." He criticized a European and American "erosion of religion, or rather the idea of personal responsibility, so that the idea of collective guilt has taken root."[13] But, in response to questions, he was vague in his self-positioning, saying only that he followed a supposed "Greco-Roman-Judeo-Christian tradition of individual responsibility."[14]

Bauer has his reasons for not going further. He has spent a lifetime in economics, not theology. He argues strongly for a division of positive and normative economics, and contends that much mischief has resulted from a mixing of the two. In response to one attempt to probe his religious belief, Bauer answered with a smile, "I have enough problems doing what I'm doing. If I went into that [theological discussion], I'd have another set of problems."[15] But that refusal to go deeper, even when made by a person as delightful and courageous as P. T. Bauer, is insufficient: Without wading into the second set of problems (the theology), there are no comprehensive answers for the first set (the economics). Bauer can tersely offer a first step to take—"Stop foreign aid. The rotten governments will fall"[16]—but not a firm second step. He can expose the lack of justice and freedom in many societies, but he does not offer great hope.

THE BOOK OF HOPE

What the Villars consultation affirmed is that hope comes from the Bible, not from the theories of man. We could see that useful programs will not emerge unless they are based on the understanding that the Bible is God's Word, inspired and authoritative for life in all its aspects, both in "spiritual" matters and in questions of economy, social ethics and public policy. For that reason we spent considerable time at the consultation assessing some contemporary attempts to turn the Bible into a document of class warfare rather than hope for all. Such twisting is not easy, but in looking at the Gospels, for example, some people make much of Jesus' "class solidarity" with the poor because of His birth in a manger, His parents' poverty, His choosing as disciples some economically marginal individuals from the despised region of Galilee, His refusal to accumulate property or wealth, and so on (Luke 2; Matt. 4).

A conference talk by Otto de Bruijne[17] was very useful

in this respect. De Bruijne noted that in behavior, claims, acts, and teachings Jesus chose to appear as He did not out of sheer solidarity with the poor (although He clearly had compassion for all those in distress) but out of a desire to be independent of powerful interests. It was important that Jesus walk freely, without economic or political strings attached. His symbolic poverty revealed the rejection of worldly attachment—"The Son of Man has no place to lay his head" (Matt. 8:20)—in order to point man to issues of lie and truth, life and death. Jesus opposed the power-hunger of the religious "wolves" and political "foxes" of his time (Matt. 7:15; Luke 13:32) and demanded of Himself and His disciples complete trust in God (Matt. 10:10, 14).

If we read in context Jesus' words, they emphasize freedom in a far more profound way than that put forward by liberation theologians. De Bruijne pointed out that Jesus' proclamation in Nazareth (Luke 4:18, 19), His blessings of the poor and woes to the rich (Luke 6:20-26), His warning against the deceitfulness of wealth (Matt. 13:22), and His exhortation that the rich cannot easily enter the kingdom (Matt. 19:23) all stand in the great tradition of the Scriptures: Wealth is a blessing for the righteous but a trap for those who put their trust in it, since wealth cannot save.[18]

The real issue, in the New Testament as well as in the Old, is not accumulation of money but use of power: How do those entrusted by God with riches or influence use those gifts to rescue their neighbors from spiritual and economic enslavement? Those who use power to gain more wealth through injustice, and do not repent, stand condemned (Ezek. 22:27; Job 24; Amos 2:6, 7; 5:12; Mark

12:40; Luke 16:19-31). The real goal, in the New Testament as in the Old, is not destructive revolution but renewal and conversion. (Jesus' approach to Zacchaeus in Luke 19 is one example of the pattern.)

Always, as de Bruijne pointed out, Jesus taught His disciples to *give* of their time, their money, and their love (Luke 6:30-38; Acts 20:35). Giving presumes having, and giving freely assumes that the owner is using his discretion. In the New Testament, the greatest need for stewardly use of God's gifts came after Pentecost, when thousands of new believers, perhaps mostly aged people, were in desperate need. The Holy Spirit urged wealthy members to sell some of their property so that the new Christians could see in physical terms the spiritual changes that Christ's sacrifice had wrought (Acts 4:34, 35). There was no coercion; when Ananias and Sapphira approached an opportunity for self-sacrifice in a legalistic way and were then punished by God for their hypocrisy, Peter explicitly noted that Ananias had owned the property and could have done what he wanted with the proceeds (Acts 5:3, 4).

The New Testament church cared for the physical needs of its members, but those needs did not expand to the point where the diaconal structure was overwhelmed and the state was asked to come in with bread and circuses. The reason, apparently, was an emphasis on working and giving. Paul warned the Thessalonians not to be idle, and used his own work of tent-making to set an example of self-reliance: "If a man will not work, he shall not eat" (2 Thess. 3:6-14). That economic strategy was so successful that when legitimate needs did arrive in the poor Jerusalem church, believers at other churches were wealthy enough to give freely of the bounty God had given them, after having already set aside enough to take care of their familial obligations.

In that situation, as in others, Paul's model of self-reliance took after Jesus' independent way of caring for His needs. We show that we are made after God's image by using liberty and creativity to provide for ourselves and our families, including aged parents (Mark 7:9-15; 1 Tim. 5:8). Sometimes tragedies can happen, but to be a long-term, dependent beggar is to go against the identity of man created in the image of God. Jesus' disciples were not to stand around begging, but to leave a town when inhabitants did not immediately recognize the importance of their work by supporting it spiritually and physically. As de Bruijne noted, over and over again the Bible shows that there is no genuine giving without self-reliance, based upon private property, at the disposal of the giver, earned by work, investment, or inheritance (a recognition of the work of forefathers).

THE CHALLENGE OF APPLICATION

The application of this thinking to international relief and development activities is crucial. The New Testament does not propose redistribution of wealth and forced "equality" for all. Instead, the emphasis is on independence from enslaving powers, spiritual or physical. God gives human beings, organized in families, the commission to "till the earth" and to subdue it. When we follow that command, we generally have the plenty that allows us to tide over our neighbors next door or around the world, until they can get back on their feet. But those who are poor have to want to get on their feet, and those who are blessed have to be willing to go throughout the world to make disciples of all nations.

What precisely do the poor of Brazil and Bangladesh, or the reporters on the Milwaukee *Journal* who write about them, need to be taught? Under the guidance of Udo Middelmann we spent considerable time at Villars discussing the essence of a Biblical worldview concerning international relief and development. Five points of understanding seem essential in helping us to go beyond a critique of obstacles and toward a proclamation of hope.

First, as Middelmann explained, the Bible shows the nature of God in relation to His creation. We gain hope for relief and development work by seeing that God is the intelligent Creator of the universe, above nature and not part of it. Pagan gods generally are *in* nature, and their messages come through nature's fertility or failure; attempts to take dominion over nature may make them angry. God's transcendence, though, means that nature itself is not a god to be feared or worshiped, but a work of God to be admired and managed.[19]

Second, Middelmann noted that the Bible shows us the nature of man in relation to God. We have hope when we see that man is created after God's image and is therefore also above nature, capable of giving nature a human shape rather than waiting to see how it shapes us. Man can be active in world development, not a gawking onlooker, nor a person fearful of angering various gods of nature. Man does not have to live passively at the edge of disaster, but can do *more* than is necessary to survive, without fear of offending Baals or other gods within nature. Without fear we can develop the surplus that helps us provide for widows and orphans and keeps us going through unfruitful seasons and lean years. Without fear of retribution by gods of nature we can dig wells, as Abraham and Isaac did. (Jealous and fearful Philistines later covered up the wells.) Without fear we can follow God's injunctions and look under the earth for iron and copper, rather than just settling for what is immediately visible (Deut. 8:3).

Third, the Bible shows us the nature of history. We have hope in that God is the Lord of history, standing above it and therefore able to intervene in it. History, moving toward both deliverance for individuals and the final redemption of the world, has a linear pattern.[20] On an individual level we are created in God's image and can stand apart from our past; following repentance we can head in a radically different direction. The whole world will finally be redeemed, and is not merely going through endless cycles of repetition. For both individuals and societies Christianity is a religion of change: Under grace we *can* strive and see positive results, "for God did not give us a spirit of timidity, but a spirit of power, of love and of self-discipline" (2 Tim. 1:7).

Fourth, Middelmann showed how the Bible gives us hope through providing a theology of individual freedom. The Protestant Reformation principle of *sola scriptura*, the Bible only, indicates that we must seek the face of the Lord as we read the Bible, whether or not our neighbors go along with us. In most societies the group, clan, or community is king, and the individual must not strive too hard or be too different, lest he upset the solidarity of the group. That fear of stepping out alone holds back societies spiritually and economically, for exceptional individuals hide their lights under bushels. Biblically, however, groups frequently are challenged. When an entire nation stumbled into apostasy, Elijah stood alone. (He did not know, until it was revealed to him, that others also had asserted their independence under God.) When Peter faltered under community pressure, Paul challenged him. The Bible frees individuals from slavery to society as it enables us to truly serve others.

Fifth, the Bible through its emphasis on the importance of just law gives us hope that we will be able to lead peaceful lives. Law's special function is not to restrict honest initiative, but to limit arbitrary power and class-based law, whether it benefits rich or poor (Exod. 12:49; Deut. 16:19). Many specific Biblical legal applications indicate that law is intended to free, not enslave. Courts, for example, were instituted in all cities (Deut. 16:18), so that justice is accessible; a requirement to come to a central city for justice might favor those with more money or time. Similarly, lost possessions are to be restored to the rightful owner; we are not to gain personal advantage through the hard times of others (Deut. 19:4; 22:1). Again, when accusations are made, witnesses are required, because truth is more important than the word of the generalissimo (Deut. 19:15). Fixed punishments for transgressors keep arbitrary justice from bringing back favoritism and unpredictability.

At the Villars consultation we recognized that, with hope through a Biblical understanding of God, man, history, freedom, and law, we can develop new ways of dealing with international relief and development questions. We have hope when we see that deprivation is not natural, and is instead the result of the unnatural entry of sin into the world. Other religions urge acceptance of the problems of the world. Buddha shut his eyes to the pain of human life. Jesus, however, wept over Jerusalem, and then died to break the power of sin. Thus we have the opportunity to bring real help to a broken world, in anticipation of the final victory over sin and death when Christ returns in power and glory.

We have new hope when we develop a changed attitude toward work. Biblically, work is valuable, not just suffering born of necessity. The Fall makes work harder and often less productive, but nowhere does the Bible state that the only reason for work is survival. After all, Adam before the Fall had the vital work and high calling of naming and gardening. The fourth commandment is not only the Sabbath commandment but the work commandment; it emphasizes that we should work six days a week, regardless of economic necessity, because work is our major activity in life, our chief opportunity to use creativity.

As Middelmann pointed out, the Biblical view of work is a remarkable contrast to that of pagan religions. Many of the latter often see work as something done by many to support the priesthood of the few, which is the only truly significant activity in society. The Bible, however, gives greatest praise not to those who contemplate but to all who work to take godly dominion over the world. For example, the positive aspects of Solomon's reign included the planting of cedar trees in the foothills so they became as plentiful as sycamores (1 Kings 10:27). Spiritual leaders did not consider themselves above hard material work: Amos also "took care of sycamore trees" (Amos 7:14), and Paul made tents.

The Bible gives us new hope to escape poverty because its stress on individual responsibility includes economic as well as spiritual components. The goal is freedom from communal dependence, including freedom from market controls. Chapters such as Leviticus 15 and Genesis 13 stress individual responsibility in choosing how to use resources of time and land.[21] Choices have consequences— for example, failure to help the poor results in God's condemnation—but freedom is vital. Dishonesty is disallowed—for example, use of just measures and weights is essential (Lev. 19:35)—but the Bible never proposes governmental or ecclesiastical establishment of wages or prices.[22]

The Biblical emphasis on work, and on honoring the fruits of work, leads to protection of private property; what we gain through our own rightful efforts is ours to use for God's glory. Those who gain wealth unjustly and do not repent are condemned, but the Bible often states that wealth is a blessing for the righteous, and that poverty is not to be romanticized (Gen. 13:2; 14:23; 1 Kings 3:13; 1 Chron. 29:12; Prov. 3:16; 8:18; 22:4). At the same time, the Bible gives us hope that those who prosper also will be charitable, not out of coercion but because individuals made after the image of a merciful God should also be merciful. Individuals who gain property are encouraged to help support widows, orphans, and others who are impoverished through no fault of their own. Individuals financially blessed by God who do not use riches to rescue others from suffering are slaves to sin (Luke 16:19-31).

Biblical wisdom gives us the opportunity to avoid economic warring on each other. Biblically, there are no superior and inferior classes; wealth can become a snare, but the real question is not just money but power. The Bible, in its emphasis on the individual, does not draw class generalizations. Some who are poor in material may be poor in spirit, but not all. Some who are rich may love their wealth, but not all. It could be said that there *is* class warfare in the Bible, but it is a war of spiritual classes, not material classes, and if we mix up the two we are mixing Christianity with paganism.

The Bible gives us the opportunity to use our freedom well by not leaving us to wander aimlessly among a variety of conflicting social principles. Instead, God throughout the Bible explains to us what our human nature is, and gives us institutions that conform to it. Chief among these, since God created us male and female, is the institution of marriage and family as basic order for society, to be sustained by all our economic and developmental policies. We are supposed to leave father and mother and form new families; there is personal freedom combined with love and continuity. A variety of ideological and political systems may be acceptable, but those that try to do away with man's God-given nature are unacceptable in theory and folly in practice.

The greatest hope of all is that God has made us members of His family, as adopted sons. That returns us to the idea of covenant. We are sons—and what father, when his son asks for sustenance, will not provide it? As Jesus said, "I am the bread of life. He who comes to me will never go hungry, and he who believes in me will never be thirsty" (John 6:35).

BACK TO ETHIOPIA

What we saw more clearly at Villars was that in the twentieth century all of our thinking, Christian and non-Christian, tends to be influenced—not controlled, but influenced—by philosophical materialism. Some have seen through Marxist glasses, with Lenin and Stalin hailed as the new Moses and Joshua. Others, such as the singers in the hit tune of 1985, "We Are the World," have seen the goal of poverty-fighting as turning stones into bread.[23] Many Christians, sincerely desiring to follow Christ, have mounted massive relief efforts, not always sure where funds are going, but sincerely convinced of the necessity of doing something, anything, that has the promise of alleviating hunger.

The Biblical view is different from most twentieth-century thought. Biblically, man is imprisoned not just by poverty but by deeper levels of alienation, imprisonment and enslavement. The ultimate alienation is the alienation of man from God—which in turn affects everything else. This is not to deemphasize the economic. People need food. People need medicine. Salvation, repentance, healing, and restoration have visible aspects, with Christ's sacrifice and our acceptance of it altering all physical, psychological, social, and economic aspects of life. But Christ's goal is a total spiritual reorientation, which will then have outworkings in all areas of life. Emphasizing the material is an easy way out, and alliances with Satan in the belief that they will help us defeat Satan are the fruits of delusion.

The titles of magazine articles conveyed the materialist version of the 1984-85 Ethiopia story: *Time* wrote of "The politics of famine; A ruthless regime compounds the plight of the starving," and *Newsweek* wrote of "The deadly politics of African aid efforts."[24] Neither magazine, however, showed understanding of the theology underlying political terror, a theology proclaiming that the state is God and that men must worship other men. Magazine story titles in

1987 continued to describe "Ethiopia's murderous transformation" or "A state of permanent revolution; Ethiopia bleeds red,"[25] but the authors could offer no hope.

What can Christians do? Many in the West want to help, but it is still not clear that we can, except in very limited ways. Ethiopians die in the spotlight, and victims of other ungodly governments die in hidden corners around the world. It is hard to be optimistic unless something changes.

But something already has changed.

Jesus Christ broke the power of sin and death nearly two thousand years ago. What does this mean today for those who are caught in bondage to suffering, sin, and death? At Christmas in 1987, as we saw new pictures of starvation, we also hailed the Heaven-born Prince of Peace and sang, "Light and life to all He brings,/ Risen with healing in His wings./ Mild He lays His glory by,/ Born that man no more may die,/ Born to raise the sons of earth,/ Born to give them second birth./ Hark, the herald angels sing, 'Glory to the new-born King.' "

Something already has changed. If the good news gets through and is taken to heart, residents of Ethiopia and other poor countries can have new spiritual birth as well as new physical hope. Through God's grace, we in the West can help—by no longer aiding their oppressors, and by making disciples as we show how the whole gospel of God meets the needs of the whole person. Through the teaching of a Biblical worldview we can be God's agents in helping to set people free from destructive attitudes and patterns of culture.

The Villars consultation was just the beginning of a process designed to change our own thinking and that of others. The Villars statement that follows is a Christmas, a beginning. Winter follows Christmas, and often it seems long. But the destination of the Villars process, and the hope of those in need throughout the world, is Easter. "He is risen," Russian Christians tell each other on Easter morning, and then wait for the customary response: "He is risen, indeed."

This is the message of Villars—Christ is risen! And because He lives, we have a transforming message of hope that touches every area of life both now and for eternity.

THE VILLARS STATEMENT ON RELIEF AND DEVELOPMENT

PREAMBLE

In the spring of 1987, a group of forty evangelical Christians from around the world gathered in Villars, Switzerland, to examine the topic of "Biblical Mandates for Relief and Development." For five days, we engaged in intense discussion, debate, and private reflection, our energies focused by a number of prepared study papers. As a result of our consultation, we who gathered at Villars have the concerns enumerated below. We encourage other believers to consider these issues in light of the Scriptures and their revelance for implementing Biblical relief and development.

A WORLD IN NEED

The extent of hunger and deprivation around the world is a reality haunting modern times. Confronted with disaster, disease, and chronic poverty, relief and development agencies have provided massive material assistance. Yet for all the resources expended, hunger and deprivation appear to be increasing. The sad reality is that so much effort has produced little in long-term results.

This reality calls us as Christians to reassess the work of relief and development in light of God's Holy Word. It is our conclusion that the consistent application of Biblical teaching will require a reorientation of relief and development practices, and that this may involve a change in our understanding of human need and in strategies to relieve suffering.

"Relief and development" is an expression that recognizes two Biblical principles. *Relief* refers to the insistence in both Testaments that the people of God must help the hungry and oppressed. *Development* stems from the Biblical vision of a people exercising their proper stewardship of God's gifts—of societies that are productive, healthy, and governed justly. Together relief and development envision substantial improvement in economic and human well-being.

We acknowledge our own sinfulness and fallibility, and we recognize that other committed Christians may not agree with all our convictions. Nevertheless, we are compelled by God's Word and by the reality of human suffering to share our convictions with Christians and others. We do not claim to have spoken the final word. Thus we offer the following conclusions of the Villars consultation for research, dialogue, and open debate among all who claim Christ as Lord.

ISSUES OF CONCERN

With this as our goal, we raise our concerns over the following issues:

1. The failure to operate from a distinctively Biblical perspective in both methods and goals.

2. The tendency to focus on meeting material needs without sufficient emphasis on spiritual needs.

3. The attempt to synthesize Marxist categories and Christian concepts, to equate economic liberation with salvation, and to use the Marxist critique, without recognizing the basic conflict between these views and the Biblical perspective.

4. The emphasis on redistribution of wealth as the answer to poverty and deprivation without recognizing the value of incentive, opportunity, creativity, and economic and political freedom.

5. The attraction to centrally controlled economies and coercive solutions despite the failures of such economies and their consistent violation of the rights of the poor.

6. A disproportionate emphasis on changing structures without recognizing the frequency with which this only exchanges one oppressive structure for another.

7. The danger of utopian and ideological entrapment, whether from the left or the right.

8. Neglecting to denounce oppression when it comes from one end or the other of the political spectrum.

9. Focusing on *external* causes of poverty in exploitation and oppression without confronting those *internal* causes that are rooted in patterns of belief and behavior within a given culture.

10. The need to make conversion and discipleship an essential component of Christian relief and development work, and to carry this out in conjunction with the local church.

11. The need to apply the teaching of the Bible as a whole in the areas of personal life, family, and work, but equally in the shaping of the culture and social life.

12. The need to reaffirm the Biblical support for the family as the basic social and economic unit and its right to own and control property, and to stand against any ideology that would diminish the family's proper role in any of these areas.

13. The need to oppose a false understanding of poverty which makes poverty itself a virtue, or which sanctifies those who are poor on the basis of their poverty.

BIBLICAL PERSPECTIVE

In response to these issues we draw attention to the following Biblical teaching and its implications for relief and development:

1. God created mankind in His own image, endowing man with freedom, creativity, significance, and moral discernment. Moreover, prior to the Fall man lived in har-

mony with all of God's creation, free from pain, suffering, and death.

2. The devastating reality of sin and evil (hunger, oppression, deprivation, disease, death, and separation from God) is the result of man's rebellion against God, which began at the Fall and continues through history.

3. The causes of hunger and deprivation, therefore, are spiritual as well as material and can only be dealt with adequately insofar as the spiritual dimension is taken into account.

4. Man's rebellion against God affects every aspect of human existence. The Fall resulted in God's curse on creation and in destructive patterns of thought, culture, and relationships, which keep men and women in bondage to poverty and deprivation.

5. The work of Christian relief and development, therefore, must involve spiritual transformation, setting people free from destructive attitudes, beliefs, values, and patterns of culture. The proclamation of the gospel and the making of disciples, then, is an unavoidable dimension of relief and development work—not only for eternal salvation, but also for the transformation of culture and economic life.

6. When people were held in bondage to hunger and deprivation by unjust social structures, the Bible consistently denounced those who perpetuated such oppression and demanded obedience to God's law. The Bibli-

cal emphasis, then, is not on "sinful structures" but rather on sinful human choices that perpetuate suffering and injustice.

7. God's ultimate answer for suffering and deprivation is the gift of His only Son, Jesus Christ, who broke the power of sin and death by His own death and resurrection. The decisive victory was won on the cross in the atoning death of Christ for all who would believe Him. The final victory will be accomplished when Christ returns in power and glory to reign with His people. Until that time all who claim Jesus as their Lord are called to care for those in need as the Holy Spirit enables them and to share the only message of true hope for a broken world.

CONCLUSION

Therefore, in light of the issues raised and the Biblical perspective outlined here, we encourage research, dialogue, and debate among all who claim Christ as Lord, so that we may serve Him more faithfully and work together more effectively.

We encourage you to send your response and your concerns to:

Villars Continuing Committee
P.O. Box 26253
Santa Ana, CA 92799-6253

The Villars Statement was signed by the following Villars consultation participants:

David M. Adams
Trans World Radio

Howard F. Ahmanson
Fieldstead & Company

Roberta Green Ahmanson
Fieldstead & Company

Theodore Baehr
Good News Communications

Clarence Bass
Bethel Theological Seminary

Charles Bennett
Food for the Hungry,
International

Pierre Berthoud
Faculte Libre de Theologie
Reformee

Spencer Bower
Christian Service Fellowship

Otto de Bruijne
Association of Evangelicals in
Africa and Madagascar

Phillip Butler
Interdev

David Chilton
Church of the Redeemer
Placerville, CA

Michael Cromartie
Ethics and Public Policy Center

Lane T. Dennis
Good News Publishers/
Crossway Books

Gene Dewey
United Nations, Geneva

Homer E. Dowdy
International Institute for Relief
and Development

George Grant
President, H.E.L.P. Services

Carrie Hawkins
Herbert Hawkins, Inc.

Preston Hawkins
Herbert Hawkins, Inc.

Evon Hedley
World Vision

Alan Jensen
Biblical Institute for Leadership
Development, International

Henry Jones
Spiritual Overseers Service

Stephen Paul Kennedy

Patricia D. Lipscomb
Fieldstead & Company

Ranald Macaulay
L'Abri Fellowship

Vishal Mangalwadi
Traci Community and ACRA

Rob Martin
Fieldstead & Company

Don McNally
University of Toronto

Udo W. Middelmann
International Institute for Relief
and Development

Darrow L. Miller
Food for the Hungry,
International

Gareth B. Miller
Farms International

Ken Myers
Berea Publications

Ronald H. Nash
Western Kentucky University

Brian P. Newman

Marvin Olasky
University of Texas at Austin

Marvin Padgett
Logos of Nashville

Clark Pinnock
McMaster Divinity College

Herbert Schlossberg

Allen R. Seeland
AGW Group, International

Susumu Uda
Kyoritsu Christian Institute for
Theological Studies and Mission

Tetsunao Yamamori
Food for the Hungry,
International

(Names of organizations are for identification only and are not meant to imply organizational commitment to the statement.)

N O T E S

CHAPTER ONE *Is There a Way Out?*

1. Austin *American-Statesman,* November 29, 1987, p. C1.
2. *Ibid.* Also see *Time,* December 21, 1987, pp. 34-45.
3. Quoted in Peter Gill, *A Year in the Death of Africa* (London: Paladin Grafton Books, 1986), p. 141.
4. *Time,* December 21, 1987, p. 44.
5. *Ibid.,* p. 43.
6. *Ibid.,* p. 44.

CHAPTER TWO *Prophet and Covenant*

1. Along with such doxologies (5:8 and 9:5, 6) Amos repeatedly sets his oracles within the wider covenant of creation, and does not restrict his prophecy to Israel and Judah (1; 2:3). It should be noted that the Lord, in bringing action against Israel, summons the fortresses of Philistia and Egypt as witnesses to the evil in Samaria (3:9). Amos also announces the universal dimension of the restoration to be introduced by the Messiah (9:11, 12).
2. The Westminister Catechism goes into this very well; many editions are available, including one published by W. Blackwood, Edinburgh and London, 1963, p. 55.
3. The verb *"bara,"* to create, is used only with God as subject. It is used forty-nine times in the Old Testament (mainly in Genesis, Isaiah and the Psalms). In Genesis 1, it occurs at three crucial points of God's creative activity: the creation of all things (1:1), of the animal world (1:20ff.), and of man (1:26ff.). This concept reminds us that God is the ultimate being. He has made all things out of nothing by the power of His word.

149

4. Paul is quoting from the Sicilian poet Aratus (Phoenomena) and from Cleanthes ("Hymn to Zeus").

5. Looking at Biblical use of some key words is important here. *"Body"* stresses the historical and external associations that influence the life of man; *"flesh"* calls to mind man's relationship to nature and mankind as a whole—it is never used of God; *"spirit"* denotes man endowed with power who has a relationship with the Spirit of God; *"soul"* stresses the individuality and the vitality of man, and draws attention to the inner life and feelings as well as to personal consciousness; *"heart"* is associated with the intellectual, volitional and emotional activities of man. This term is only used of God and man.

6. To stress the unique identity of man as he stands before the Creator, the Bible uses the following terms: soul *(nefesh, neshma)*; spirit *(ruah)*; heart *(leb)*. This, of course, does not deny the great variety of usages these words can have in other contexts. For further discussion and bibliography see my article "L'homme, la mort et la vie: perspectives bibliques," in *La Revue Reformee*, No. 149, 1987, pp. 12-23.

7. Word usage in Genesis and later in the Bible is important: *radah* means to tread (in the wine press, Joel 4:13) and by extension, to rule, govern (Ps. 72:8). *Kabash* means to subject someone, to make subservient (Jer. 34:16; Num. 32:22) and to violate or rape (Esth. 7:8). Because of the reality of evil in the midst of our world one can notice an ambivalence in the way these terms may be used, both for good or evil.

8. *'Abad* means to work, to cultivate, to serve, but also to serve in the Temple and thus to adore.

9. *Shamar* means to guard, to watch over, to protect, to save (Gen. 41:35; Ps. 121:7).

10. Atrahasis, Tablet I, has man created in order to relieve the gods from the heavy and arduous work that was their lot. See W. G. Lambert and A. R. Millard, eds., *The Babylonian Story of the Flood* (London: Oxford University Press, 1969), p. 42ff. The Fall, of course, had drastic affects on work, procreation, and other aspects of the creation. Alienation resulting from the Fall will continue to have an effect until the return of Christ, but until that time we have God's mandate to glorify Him in our work.

11. The NIV translates "city." In Josh. 13:23, this word is used in conjunction with another word meaning a "permanent settlement

without wall; farm; village." It is therefore preferable to speak of a "permanent settlement."

12. For example, at Ugarit, the skill and art of the blacksmith were attributed to the divinity *Ktrwhss*.

13. In Genesis 2 and 3, the tree of the knowledge of good and evil represents man's autonomous knowledge that rejects the sovereignty of God. By choosing autonomy, man seeks to become his own end. He seeks to establish knowledge, values and happiness on a purely horizontal level. It is the beginning of idolatry: the creature becoming the reference point. In fact, man is placed before two different attitudes towards life, two different world and life views. The battle, it should be noted, is not between faith and knowledge, but between two different forms of knowledge, one whose foundation is God and the other man. The former brings wisdom, integrity and life; the latter brings folly, ruin and death. Which one will man choose?

14. Consider within such a perspective Isa. 54:10 and Matt. 5:45.

15. The reason for this restriction lies in the fact that the blood is associated with the life of the animal and that it has an important place in the ritual of atonement (Gen. 3:21; 4:4), as the book of Leviticus reveals (Lev. 1:5; 3:17; 7:26; 17:12; 19:26).

16. M. H. Segal: *The Pentateuch* (Jerusalem: Magnes Press, 1976), p. 23.

17. The Biblical legislation is often given within an historical setting (Lev. 10; 24:10-16; Num. 15:32-36) and can have a prophetic dimension (Deut. 17:14-20). The historical as well as the ethical and religious justifications appeal to conscience and have an educational character to motivate obedience (Exod. 6:7-9, 20-25).

18. The one exception to the principle of equal justice for all was the case of the slave. But it must be noted that the relevant legislation seeks to protect and to preserve the dignity of the slave: his condition is temporary; he must not become the object of abusive physical violence; he must be treated as a human being (Deut. 23:15).

19. With one notable exception: Deuteronomy 25:11, 12.

20. For further discussion, see Sh. M. Paul, *Studies in the Book of the Covenant in the Light of Cuneiform and Biblical Law* (Leiden: E. J. Brill, 1970), pp. 27-42, and A. van Selms, *"Law" in New Bible Dictionary* (London: Intervarsity Press, 1962), p. 720.

21. Orphir especially, which roughly corresponds with present-day Somalia (2 Kings 14:22; 2 Chron. 26:2; 1 Kings 9:26).

22. A. Neher, *Amos* (Paris: Vrin, 1981), p. 207.
23. Including copper-mining in the Arabah. J. Bright mentions weaving and dyeing at Debir; see his *History of Israel* (London: S.C.M. Press, 1974), p. 256.
24. 2 Chronicles 26:10.
25. Amos 3:12. The meaning of the Hebrew is uncertain.
26. N. Avigad, "Samaria," in *Encyclopedia of Archaeological Excavations in the Holy Land,* Vol. 4 (London: Oxford University Press, 1978), p. 1046.
27. The difference between the two cults was that the former was agrarian and the latter Dionysiac.
28. The burning deprived Edom's king of the proper burial due even to one's enemies (1 Kings 2:31; 2 Kings 9:34). In the Old Testament, the burning of a corpse is extremely rare (1 Sam. 31:12) and is probably a sign of God's judgment. In the case of Saul and his sons (1 Sam. 31:12), it has been suggested that cremation was performed to prevent any further abuse of the bodies. In Leviticus 21:9, burning is the legal penalty for prostitution (*cf.* also Gen. 38:24).
29. A. Neher, *op. cit.,* pp. 52, 53.
30. A. Motyer, *The Day of the Lion: The Message of Amos* (Leicester: Intervarsity Press, 1974).
31. A. Neher, *op. cit.,* p. 50.
32. This inclination to turn away from the law is well illustrated by the king himself. Uzziah sought to claim for himself a privilege that was reserved for the high priest. We are told in the book of Chronicles that "after Uzziah became powerful, his pride led to his downfall. He was unfaithful to the Lord his God, and entered the temple of the Lord to burn incense" (2 Chron. 26:16). Those words "his pride" mean literally, "his heart was exalted"; he had high aims. "He was unfaithful to God" means "he acted counter to his duty towards God." This incident kindled the conflict which seemed to exist in Jerusalem between the king and the clergy. (The priest-Levites had saved the Davidic dynasty from the hands of Athaliah— 2 Chron. 22:10-12, and the influence they exercised probably weighed on the king.)
33. There was a difference: Pagan gods stood *on* the calves or bulls, while in Jeroboam's religion there was no representation of God standing on the statues. The syncretism and confusion were all the more subtle!
34. Mosaic law allowed servitude; it was a means of paying one's debt

by labor. However, the term of bondage was limited and the slaves were to be treated as hired workers (Exod. 21:1, 2; Lev. 25:39-43; Deut. 15:1-11). Amos and others testified that the practice was abused (2 Kings 4:1; Neh. 5:5).

35. In Amos 2:6, the "righteous" are the innocent party in a trial, while the "needy" are the weak, the defenseless. In Amos 8:6, a parallel passage, the word "poor" is used in the place of "righteous."

36. Paul is quoting from Isaiah 22:13. As the people of Jerusalem faced the coming judgment announced by Isaiah, rather than recognizing their unfaithfulness, repenting of their sins, and returning to the Lord, they preferred to make the best of the present joys of life, thinking that is all it has to offer.

37. These gains were obtained by the breaking of the laws protecting the powerless (Exod. 22:26, 27; Deut. 24:12, 13, 17) or by exorbitant claims or false charges of damage.

38. It should be noted that Baal itself is not mentioned once in Amos. The cult that Jeroboam introduced in Israel after Solomon's reign, and that Jehu restored, was not overtly idolatrous. Rather, it was an appeal to tradition, a breaking of the law, and an integration of idolatry.

39. The Greek translation of the Old Testament, and the New Testament, offer a different reading of verse 12, one that gives it a messianic dimension: "So that the remnant of men and all the nations that bear my name may seek the Lord" (Acts 15:17). James considers this passage as a proof that Jesus is the Messiah!

CHAPTER THREE *The Controlled Economy*

1. From the official Nobel announcement of the Royal Academy of Sciences, *Swedish Journal of Economics,* Vol. 76, No. 4, December 1974.

2. Gunnar Myrdal, *Asian Drama: An Inquiry into the Poverty of Nations,* 3 vols., Vol. 1 (New York: Pantheon, 1968), p. 52. Perhaps he did not recognize the irony in applying to his ideal the name commonly given to its adversary, the revival of evangelical Christianity in the same century.

3. Gunnar Myrdal, *Beyond the Welfare State* (1960), quoted in John C. O'Brien, "Gunnar Myrdal and the Moral Philosopher," *International Journal of Social Economics,* Vol. 9, No. 4, 1982.

4. *Asian Drama,* Vol. 1, p. 54.

5. *Ibid.*, p. 118.
6. *Ibid.*, p. 131.
7. *Ibid.*, p. 309. But note the qualifying phrase, "[i]n our cultural setting . . ."
8. *Ibid.*, pp. v, viii. This passage is a fascinating study in ideological positioning: "I find myself in complete agreement with the basic and traditional values which I once defined as the 'American Creed,' the radical ideals of the Enlightenment to which America has conservatively adhered." In a single sentence describing his position, Myrdal uses the terms "basic," "traditional," "radical," and "conservative."
9. *Ibid.*, p. 65.
10. *Ibid.*, Vol. 2, pp. 713ff., 865ff.
11. *Ibid.*, Vol. 1, p. 295.
12. *Ibid.*, p. 300.
13. Eugene R. Dykema, "No View Without a Viewpoint: Gunnar Myrdal," *World Development*, Special Issue, Vol. 14, No. 2, February 1986, p. 150.
14. Myrdal, *Asian Drama*, Vol. 3, p. 1964ff.
15. O'Brien, "Gunnar Myrdal and the Moral Philosopher," p. 3.
16. Dykema, "No View Without a Viewpoint," p. 160.
17. *Asian Drama*, Vol. 1, p. 28.
18. *Ibid.*, Vol. 3, p. 1941.
19. *Ibid.*, Vol. 2, p. 710.
20. *Ibid.*, Vol. 1, p. 434ff.
21. *Ibid.*, Vol. 2, p. 925.
22. *Ibid.*, Vol. 3, pp. 1547, 1550.
23. *Ibid.*, Vol. 1, pp. 35, 185, 228.
24. *An International Economy,* p. 51ff.
25. *Asian Drama*, Vol. 1, p. 699.
26. *Ibid.*, p. 257.
27. *Ibid.*, p. 35ff.
28. *Ibid.*, p. 11. His faith in education can be quite extravagant. Here he asserts that it brought about de-Stalinization in the U.S.S.R.
29. *Ibid.*, Vol. 3, p. 1696.
30. *Ibid.*, Vol. 2, p. 728.
31. *An International Economy,* p. 300ff.
32. *Asian Drama*, Vol. 1, p. 294.
33. *Ibid.*, pp. 63, 112.
34. *Asian Drama*, Vol. 2, pp. 1057, 1064-1067, 1078, 1081ff., 1124-1131, 1241ff., 1294, 1296ff.

35. *Ibid.,* Vol. 1, p. 91.
36. *Ibid.,* Vol. 3, pp. 1574, 1577, 1606ff.
37. *Ibid.,* p. 1692.
38. Gunnar Myrdal, *Challenge to Affluence* (New York: Pantheon Books, 1963), p. 51ff. He contrasted this with what he thought was the American hard-heartedness in funding the welfare state in so miserly a fashion. (The War on Poverty was just about to get under way.)
39. *Asian Drama,* Vol. 1, p. 61ff.
40. *Ibid.,* p. 453ff.
41. *Ibid.,* p. 278.
42. *Ibid.,* p. 303.
43. *Ibid.,* Vol. 2, pp. 977ff., 982-985.
44. *Ibid.,* Vol. 1, p. 60. Oddly, along with the other virtues of this new creation will be both "solidarity and 'free competition' in a much wider sense than the term implies in economic analysis." The "solidarity" is much easier to envision in the planner-directed society he envisages than is the free competition.
45. *Ibid.,* Vol. 2, pp. 875, 880, 891.
46. *Ibid.,* pp. 999-1003.
47. *Ibid.,* Vol. 3, p. 1622.
48. *Ibid.,* Vol. 1, p. 104.
49. *Ibid.,* pp. 104, 108.
50. *Cf. ibid.,* Vol. 3, p. 2117: "Unlike the purified doctrines on the 'higher' level, popular religion in South Asia is imbued with demonology and magic, vastly more than it ever was in Europe, at least since the early Middle Ages. This popular religion also gives sanction to a stale social and economic stratification and other non-rational elements in the national cultures. It follows that in South Asia inhibitions and obstacles to rational thinking are much greater than they had been in Europe."
51. *Ibid.,* Vol. 1, pp. 78, 103.
52. *Ibid.,* Vol. 1, p. 72ff. Emphasis added.
53. *Ibid.,* p. 114. John Kenneth Galbraith's work is full of the same opinion. See especially *The Nature of Mass Poverty* (Cambridge: Harvard Univ. Press, 1979), pp. 61ff., 93, 100ff.
54. *Ibid.,* Vol. 1, p. 259.
55. *Ibid.,* Vol. 2, p. 730. This in spite of the fact that Myrdal knows that the elite are aloof from the masses, whom they despise. See *ibid.,* p. 888ff.

56. Dykema, "No View Without a Viewpoint," pp. 152ff., 161.
57. *Asian Drama*, Vol. 2, p. 709.
58. Myrdal, *An International Economy*, pp. 21-24.
59. *Ibid.*, p. 256ff.
60. *Ibid.*, p. 200ff.
61. *Challenge to Affluence*, p. 62.
62. *Ibid.*, p. 69.
63. *Asian Drama*, Vol. 2, p. 735ff.
64. *An International Economy*, p. 112.
65. *Challenge to Affluence*, p. 94.
66. *Asian Drama*, Vol. 2, pp. 756-776.
67. *Ibid.*, Vol. 1, p. 145ff.
68. *Ibid.*, p. 448.
69. *Asian Drama*, Vol. 1, p. 623ff. The problem of the missing investors seems to be that they have the distressing tendency to desire the return of their capital.
70. *Ibid.*, pp. 634-637.
71. *Ibid.*, p. 67.
72. *Ibid.*, Vol. 2, pp. 779, 868ff., 879.
73. *Ibid.*, Vol. 1, p. 115ff.
74. *Ibid.*, Vol. 2, p. 905.
75. *Ibid.*, pp. 875, 880, 891, 895-899.
76. *Ibid.*, Vol. 3, p. 1902. The comprehensiveness of the vision and the completeness of the controls that will be required are characteristic of the twentieth-century utopias. *Cf.* Karl Mannheim, *Man and Society: In an Age of Reconstruction* (Kegan Paul, Trench, Trubner, 1940), p. 114: Planning society's future is to be done "on the basis of a thorough knowledge of the whole mechanism of society and the way in which it works. It is not the treatment of symptoms but an attack on the strategic points, fully realizing the results." This differs from Myrdal only in its complacency and tone of triumph; the Swedish economist's relative sense of realism is perhaps due to an additional quarter-century of experience with the difficulties of bringing utopia to pass.
77. *Ibid.*, pp. 1621ff., 1628ff., 1630, 1641, 1706ff.
78. *Ibid.*, Vol. 2, pp. 725-738.
79. *Ibid.*, pp. 737, 819, 853ff., 884ff.
80. *Ibid.*, pp. 909, 921, 924, 929, 931ff., 935.
81. *Ibid.*, pp. 1337ff., 1341ff.
82. *Ibid.*, p. 913.

83. *Ibid.*, pp. 941, 944ff., 946ff., 950ff., 956, 958.
84. *Ibid.*, p. 925.
85. *Ibid.*, Vol. 3, p. 2031ff.
86. Bertram Silverman, "The Crisis of the Swedish Welfare State," *Challenge*, Vol. 23, No. 3, July/August 1980, pp. 39, 41.
87. *An International Economy*, p. 301.
88. "Luncheon in Honor of Gunnar and Alva Myrdal: Response to Introduction," *American Economic Review*, May 1972, Vol. 62, No. 2, p. 459. Myrdal refers here to John Kenneth Galbraith as a "likeminded rebel." *Ibid.*, p. 461.
89. Robert L. Bartley, "A Conversation with Gunnar Myrdal," *The Wall Street Journal*, February 14, 1979, p. 20.
90. Reynolds, "Gunnar Myrdal's Contribution to Economics," p. 491.

CHAPTER FOUR *The Pursuit of Utopia*

1. Gregory Baum discusses ideology in broader terms in his book *Religion and Alienation, a Theological Reading of Sociology* (New York: Paulist Press, 1975), for example on pp. 99-111.
2. Robert P. Ericksen, *Theologians Under Hitler* (New Haven: Yale, 1985). Also Richard J. Neuhaus, "The Obligations and Limits of Political Commitment," *This World*, August 1986, pp. 55-69.
3. Solzhenitsyn, *Warning to the Western World* (London: BBC, 1986) is one of his many books. See also Robert Conquest, *The Harvest of Sorrow, Soviet Collectivization and the Terror-Famine* (Edmonton: University of Alberta Press, 1986), and Paul Johnson, *Modern Times, the World from the Twenties to the Eighties* (San Francisco: Harper & Row, 1983).
4. Sociologist Peter L. Berger has best pointed this out: *The Capitalist Revolution*, chap. 9.
5. Hollander, *Political Pilgrims, Travels of Western Intellectuals to the Soviet Union, China, and Cuba 1928-1978* (New York: Oxford University Press, 1981).
6. Lloyd Billingsley tells this story in *The Generation That Knew Not Josef, a Critique of Marxism and the Religious Left* (Portland, Ore.: Multnomah Press, 1985). It is a sobering reminder of how easily well-meaning people can be completely duped.
7. See John Eagleson, ed., *Christians and Socialism* (Maryknoll, N.Y.: Orbis, 1975), pp. 161, 163, 168, 169. The larger picture is painted by Andrew Kirk, *Liberation Theology, an Evangelical View from the*

Third World (Atlanta: John Knox, 1979) and by Deane W. Ferm, *Third World Liberation Theologies, an Introductory Survey* (Maryknoll, N.Y.: Orbis, 1986).

8. J. P. Miranda, *Communism in the Bible* (Maryknoll, N.Y.: Orbis, 1982).

9. Blase Bonpane calls on his readers to join in the armed struggle as Christians in a charming book entitled *Guerrillas for Peace, Liberation Theology and the Central American Revolution* (Boston: South End Press, 1985). For more information on the leftist involvements of these churchmen, see Ernest W. Lefever, *Amsterdam to Nairobi, the World Council of Churches and the Third World* (Washington: Ethics and Public Policy Center, 1979); Paul Seabury, "Trendier Than Thou, the Episcopal Church and the Secular World," *Harper's Magazine*, October and December 1978; and Richard J. Neuhaus, "The World Council of Churches and Radical Chic," *Worldview* 20 (1977), pp. 14-22.

10. The persistent and courageous work of Michael Bordeaux at Keston College has been pressing this scandal upon us in recent years.

11. Thomas Sowell, *Marxism, Philosophy and Economics* (New York: William Morrow, 1985), pp. 213-215; P. T. Bauer, "Western Guilt and Third World Poverty," in *Equality, the Third World, and Economic Delusions* (Boston: Harvard University Press, 1981).

12. Benjamin G. Smillie, ed., *Political Theology in the Canadian Context* (Waterloo, Ont.: Wilfred Laurier University Press, 1982). See Harry Antonides, *Stones for Bread, the Social Gospel and Its Contemporary Legacy* (Jordan Station, Ont.: Paideia Press, 1985) chap. 6.

13. Berger, *The Capitalist Revolution,* p. 208ff. He writes, "Socialism is one of the most powerful myths of the modern era; to the extent that socialism retains this mythic quality, it cannot be disconfirmed by empirical evidence in the minds of its adherents" (p. 215).

14. Jews as well as Christians are easily seduced and for much the same reasons. See Murray Friedman, *The Utopian Dilemma, American Judaism and Public Policy* (Washington, D.C.: Ethics and Public Policy Center, 1985).

15. This is the thesis of Van A. Harvey, *The Historian and the Believer* (New York: Macmillan, 1966).

16. Berger, *The Capitalist Revolution,* pp. 66-71.

17. Ernst Bloch, *The Principle of Hope* (Cambridge, Mass.: MIT Press,

1985). Let us not forget that Bloch was the inspiration for Moltmann's *Theology of Hope* (New York: Harper & Row, 1967).

18. Michael Novak places his criticism of liberation theology precisely on this issue of praxis: *Freedom with Justice, Catholic Social Thought and Liberal Institutions* (San Francisco, Calif.: Harper & Row, 1984), chap. 10. See also Novak, editor, *Liberation South, Liberation North* (Washington: American Enterprise Institute, 1981).

19. Deane William Ferm, *op. cit.,* pp. 107-115.

20. A recent example of the continuing romance with socialism even among evangelicals is Andrew Kirk, *The Good News of the Kingdom Coming* (London: Marshall, 1983).

21. Michael Novak, *The Spirit of Democratic Capitalism* (New York: Simon and Schuster, 1982); see especially part 2 ("The Twilight of Socialism"). See also Berger, *The Capitalist Revolution,* chap. 8: "Industrial Socialism: A Control Case."

22. See Sven Rydenfelt, *A Pattern for Failure, Socialist Economies in Crisis* (New York: Harcourt Brace Jovanovich, 1984), pp. 117-124.

23. See Paul Johnson's contribution to *Will Capitalism Survive?,* Ernest W. Lefever, ed. (Washington: Ethics and Public Policy Center, 1979), p. 5.

24. This is one of several unique features of Berger, *The Capitalist System,* chap. 7: "East Asian Capitalism."

25. Brian Griffiths, *The Creation of Wealth* (Downers Grove, Ill.: Inter-Varsity Press, 1984), chap. 2.

26. A call for prudence is one of the valuable features of J. Brian Benestad, *The Pursuit of a Just Social Order, Policy Statements of the US Catholic Bishops, 1966-80* (Washington: Ethics and Public Policy Center, 1982).

27. This is a central concern of Herbert Schlossberg's book, *Idols for Destruction* (Nashville: Thomas Nelson, 1983).

CHAPTER FIVE *The Free Economy*

1. P. T. Bauer, *Dissent on Development: Studies and Debates in Development Economics* (London: Weidenfeld and Nicolson, 1971), p. 221.

2. P. T. Bauer, *Reality and Rhetoric: Studies in the Economics of Development* (Cambridge: Harvard Univ. Press, 1984), pp. 1ff., 7ff., 17ff.

3. *Dissent on Development,* p. 290ff.
4. *Ibid.,* pp. 371ff., 388. See also p. 413ff.: "The obstruction of the rise of a prosperous peasantry, an inevitable outcome, has much affected the political and social landscape. The concentration of power and money in the hands of the government has increased the intensity of the political conflicts in Ghana and Nigeria."
5. *Ibid.,* p. 449ff.
6. *Ibid.,* p. 18ff.
7. *Ibid.,* p. 307.
8. *Ibid.,* p. 428ff.
9. *Ibid.,* p. 313.
10. *Ibid.,* pp. 314-323.
11. *Ibid.,* pp. 325-327. A less important issue for Bauer is the misuse of quantification techniques. He believes that much of the statistical analysis is spurious. *Ibid.,* p. 338ff. Also Bauer, *Equality, the Third World and Economic Delusion* (Cambridge: Harvard Univ. Press, 1981), p. 22.
12. *Ibid.,* p. 12ff.
13. *Dissent on Development,* p. 41.
14. *Ibid.,* p. 294ff.
15. *Ibid.,* p. 195ff.
16. *Ibid.,* p. 25.
17. *Ibid.,* pp. 34ff., 216ff., 452.
18. *Ibid.,* pp. 148ff., 158, 218, 456.
19. *Equality,* pp. 66-73.
20. *Reality and Rhetoric,* p. 80.
21. *Dissent on Development,* p. 460.
22. *Equality,* p. 16.
23. *Ibid.,* p. 44ff.; *Reality and Rhetoric,* p. 83.
24. *Dissent on Development,* pp. 74ff.
25. *Ibid.,* pp. 75-77.
26. *Ibid.,* p. 83ff.
27. *Equality,* p. 115.
28. *Dissent on Development,* pp. 327-330.
29. *Asian Drama,* Vol. 3, p. 1621.
30. *Equality,* p. 205.
31. *Ibid.,* pp. 85-89.
32. *Reality and Rhetoric,* p. 86ff.
33. *Equality,* pp. 80, 106, 176ff.
34. *Reality and Rhetoric,* pp. 19, 165 (n. 1).

35. *Ibid.,* p. 21ff.
36. *Dissent on Development,* p. 83ff.
37. E.g., *Equality,* p. 163ff.
38. *Ibid.,* p. 176ff.
39. *Dissent on Development,* pp. 100-102. Curiously, Bauer in one place asserts that we cannot know what the effects of aid are because we do not know what would have happened without it. See *ibid.,* p. 98ff. This is odd because Bauer does not hesitate to make inferences on the subject elsewhere, and they do not seem in any way forced.
40. *Equality,* p. 107.
41. *Ibid.,* p. 114.
42. *Reality and Rhetoric,* p. 22ff.
43. *Ibid.,* pp. 22ff., 30, 68ff.; *Equality,* p. 93ff.
44. *Ibid.,* p. 200ff.

CHAPTER SIX *Imperatives for Economic Development*

1. Raymond H. Brand, "At the Point of Need," *Journal of the American Scientific Affiliation,* March 1987, Vol. 39, No. 3, pp. 3-8.
2. Julian L. Simon and Herman Kahn, eds., *The Resourceful Earth: A Response to Global 2000* (Oxford: Basil Blackwell, 1984).
3. On the damage that misdirected guilt feelings do to people in poor countries see Pascal Bruckner, *The Tears of the White Man: Compassion as Contempt,* trans. William R. Beer (New York: The Free Press, 1986).
4. Pierre Berthoud's essay in chapter 2 of this book goes deeper into the prophetic view of oppression. For an example of the mistaken hermeneutic, see Nicholas Wolterstorff, "The Bible and Economics: The Hermeneutical Issues," *Transformation,* Vol. 4, Nos. 3 and 4, June-September/October-December 1987, pp. 11-19; note also the response by Herbert Schlossberg in *ibid.,* pp. 20-25. That entire double issue of *Transformation* records the papers given at the Oxford Conference on Christian Faith and Economics held at Oxford University in January 1987.
5. The desperate situation in Nyerere's Tanzania has been widely reported. See, for example, Edward Girardet, "Tanzanians Doubt 'Former' Leader Nyerere will Bring Reform," *The Christian Science Monitor,* March 21, 1986; Ken Adelman, "The Great Black Hope," *Harper's,* July 1981, pp. 14-19; David Lamb, *The Africans* (New

York: Random House, 1982), pp. 65-69; "Nyerere Strolls on Towards Never-Never Land," *The Economist,* October 20, 1984, p.
33ff.

6. Michael F. Lofchie, "The Roots of Economic Crisis in Tanzania,"
Current History, April 1985, p. 159.

7. For an argument, and considerable evidence, showing how foreign
aid has harmed people in the recipient nations see Doug Bandow,
"Foreign Aid Prescriptions," *The American Spectator,* Vol. 19, No.
9, September 1986, pp. 21-23.

8. Warren T. Brookes, *The Economy in Mind* (New York: Universe
Books, 1982), p. 224ff.

9. Interviews by the author, August 28-29, 1987.

10. See the very important book by George Gilder, *Men and Marriage*
(Gretna, La.: Pelican Publishing Company, 1986), especially chapters
6 and 8.

CHAPTER SEVEN *The Beginning of Hope*

1. Milwaukee *Journal,* December 4, 1987, p. 7A.
2. *Ibid.,* December 2, 1987, p. 7A.
3. *Ibid.,* December 4, 1987, p. 6A.
4. *Ibid.*
5. *Ibid.,* p. 7A.
6. *Ibid.,* December 2, 1987, p. 7A.
7. *Ibid.,* December 3, 1987, p. 12A.
8. *Ibid.,* p. 13A.
9. *Ibid.,* December 6, 1987, p. 3J.
10. *Ibid.*
11. *Ibid.*
12. Quoted by Jesus in the parable of the sower (Matt. 13:14; Mark
4:12; Luke 8:10).
13. Seminar, University of Texas Economics Department, December 3,
1987.
14. Seminar, December 1, 1987.
15. Author's conversation with Bauer, December 3, 1987.
16. Answer to seminar question about what Americans should do to
help impoverished Africans.
17. Association for Evangelicals in Africa and Madagascar, Nairobi.
18. See Psalms 7; 49; 52; Jeremiah 9:23.
19. The Bible turned many pagan gods from lords into servants. For

example, Genesis 1 shows that the sun and the moon are not gods or masters to be worshiped or obeyed, but objects created by God to serve man by providing light and helping us know time and seasons.

20. Middelmann points out that the holidays celebrated in various cultures indicate views of history. Biblical holidays are not reenactments of timelessness, but recognitions of God's intervention in history at particular times: Passover for a one-time exodus, Sukkot for particular wilderness wanderings. Christmas and Easter, we might add, show God's most wonderful intervention.

21. The one exception to free transfer of ownership was in land within Israel, since it was tied to the covenant with Abraham and God's plan of salvation. Land in ancient Israel could only be leased, not sold; the land itself, however, could be used according to individual initiative, and its harvest or other benefits could be exchanged.

22. The medieval church would later cause great economic harm by setting prices arbitrarily; the Biblical model is that of prices reflecting mutual consent and having enough flexibility to meet different conditions.

23. It is not clear whether those who wrote and sang the song knew that Jesus refused Satan's proposal that Jesus turn stones into bread.

24. *Time,* May 20, 1985, p. 37; *Newsweek,* June 3, 1985, p. 37.

25. *The New Republic,* July 6, 1987, p. 12; *Harper's,* January 1987, p. 53.

SCRIPTURE INDEX

SCRIPTURE INDEX

INDEX

Abortion, 121 see also *Population Control*
Abraham, 25, 26, 83, 132
Adam, 21, 22, 31, 134
Addis Ababa, 9
Africa, 10, 12, 68, 86-88, 93-95, 108, 112, 121, 126
African National Congress, 112
Amnesty International, 108
Amos, 16, 19, 20, 28, 29, 31-39, 65-67, 69, 123, 128, 134, 135, 136
Assyria, 28

Baalism, 30
Bangladesh, 119-121, 131
Bauer, P. T., 85-99, 105, 122, 125-127; *Dissent on Development*, 85; at The University of Texas, 126
Berthoud, Pierre, 122-123
Birth control see *Population Control*
Bloch, Ernst, 75, 76
Brandt Commission, 100
Brauman, Rony, 11
Brazil, 112, 113, 119, 121, 131
Bribes, 60, 106, 123
Brookes, Warren, 111
Buchanan, James, 94
Buddha, 133

Cambodia, 69
Canada, 70

Capitalism, 68, 70, 71, 77, 78, 80, 81
Central planning, 42, 53-56, 78, 92, 94, 95, 102, 107
Ceylon, 55
Chamberlain, Neville, 69
Chesterton, G. K., 116
China, 77, 79
Choice, importance of, 19, 32, 38, 116
Christmas, 14, 138, 139
Class, economic, 27, 29, 39, 68, 70, 74, 75, 77, 78, 124, 127, 133, 136
Club of Rome, 100
Corruption, 35, 59, 62, 97, 106, 108
Covenant, 2, 16, 19-21, 24-26, 28, 30-39, 122, 124, 136
Cultural factors, 49, 50, 57, 58, 62, 86, 89, 95, 112, 113, 115, 125
Cultural mandate, 22, 23, 25, 39

De Bruijne, Otto, 127-130
Dewey, John, 44
Dictatorship, 32, 124 see also *Marx*
Directed economy, 41
Dissent on Development see *Bauer*
Doctors Without Borders, 11
Dualism, 14, 22, 116

Easter, 139
Education, 47, 51, 52, 58, 74, 96
Elijah, 133

169

ABOUT THE AUTHORS

Dr. Marvin Olasky is a journalism professor at the University of Texas and the author of *Prodigal Press* and other books.

Dr. Herbert Schlossberg is the author of *Idols for Destruction* and coauthor of *Turning Point: A Christian Worldview Declaration.*

Pierre Berthoud is Professor of Old Testament and Dean of Faculty at the Faculté Libre de Théologie Reformée, Aix-en-Provence, France.

Dr. Clark Pinnock is Professor of Theology at McMaster Divinity College, Hamilton, Ontario and the author of *Reason Enough, Set Forth Your Case,* and other books.